# Auténtico **2**

## LEVELED VOCABULARY AND GRAMMAR WORKBOOK

## CORE PRACTICE

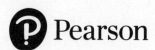 Pearson

Boston, Massachusetts • Chandler, Arizona • Glenview, Illinois • New York, New York

Pearson, 330 Hudson Street, New York, NY 10013.

ISBN-13: 978-0-328-92375-5
ISBN-10:    0-328-92375-3

4  17

# Auténtico

## 2

### LEVELED VOCABULARY AND GRAMMAR WORKBOOK

## GUIDED PRACTICE

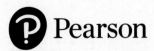 Pearson

Boston, Massachusetts • Chandler, Arizona • Glenview, Illinois • New York, New York

# Table of Contents

# Tema 6: La televisión y el cine

# Tema 7: Buen provecho

# Tema 8: Cómo ser un buen turista

# Tema 9: ¿Cómo será el futuro?

# Dear Parents and Guardians:

Learning a second language can be both exciting and fun. As your child studies Spanish, he or she will not only learn to communicate with Spanish speakers, but will also learn about their cultures and daily lives. Language learning is a building process that requires considerable time and practice, but it is one of the most rewarding things your child can learn in school.

Language learning calls on all of the senses and on many skills that are not necessarily used in other kinds of learning. Students will find their Spanish class different from other classes in a variety of ways. For instance, lectures generally play only a small role in the language classroom. Because the goal is to learn to communicate, students interact with each other and with their teacher as they learn to express themselves about things they like to do (and things they don't), their personalities, the world around them, foods, celebrations, pastimes, technology, and much more. Rather than primarily listening to the teacher, reading the text, and memorizing information as they might in a social studies class, language learners will share ideas; discuss similarities and differences between cultures; ask and answer questions; and work with others to practice new words, sounds, and sentence structures. Your child will be given a variety of tasks to do in preparation for such an interactive class. He or she will complete written activities, perform listening tasks, watch and listen to videos, and go on the Internet. In addition, to help solidify command of words and structures, time will need to be spent on learning vocabulary and practicing the language until it starts to become second nature. Many students will find that using flash cards and doing written practice will help them become confident using the building blocks of language.

To help you help your child in this endeavor, we offer the following insights into the textbook your child will be using, along with suggestions for ways that you can help build your child's motivation and confidence—and as a result, their success with learning Spanish.

## Textbook Organization

Your child will be learning Spanish using *Auténtico*, which means "authentic." The emphasis throughout the text is on learning to use the language in authentic, real ways. Chapters are organized by themes such as school life, food and health, family and celebrations, etc. At the beginning of each **Tema** (*theme*) is a section called **A ver si recuerdas**, which reviews key vocabulary and grammar from first-year Spanish as it relates to the individual theme of the upcoming chapter. Each chapter begins with **Vocabulario en contexto**, which gives an initial presentation of new grammar and vocabulary in the form of pictures, short dialogues, and audio recordings. Students then watch the new vocabulary and grammar used in an authentic context in an engaging video in the **Videohistoria**. Once students have been exposed to the new language, the **Vocabulario en uso** and **Gramática** sections offer lots of practice with the language as well as explanations of how the language works. The **Lectura, La cultura en vivo, Presentación oral,** and **Presentación escrita** sections provide activities for your child to use the language by understanding readings, giving oral or written presentations, and learning more about the cultural perspectives of Spanish speakers. The **Auténtico** section offers your child a chance to see how the language they have learned is used by native speakers in an authentic context such as a news report, talk show, or podcast. Finally, all chapters conclude with an at-a-glance review of the chapter material called **Repaso del capítulo** (*Chapter Review*), with summary lists and charts, and practice activities like those on the chapter test. If students have trouble with a given task, the **Repaso del capítulo** tells them where in the chapter they can go to review.

Here are some suggestions that will help your child become a successful language learner.

*Routine:*

Provide a special, quiet place for study, equipped with a Spanish-English dictionary, pens or pencils, paper, computer, and any other items your child's teacher suggests.

- Encourage your child to study Spanish at a regular time every day. A study routine will greatly facilitate the learning process.

*Strategy:*

- Remind your child that class participation and memorization are very important in a foreign language course.
- Tell your child that in reading or listening activities, as well as in the classroom, it is not necessary to understand every word. Suggest that they listen or look for key words to get the gist of what's being communicated.
- Encourage your child to ask questions in class if he or she is confused. Remind the child that other students may have the same question. This will minimize frustration and help your child succeed.

*Real-life connection:*

- Outside of the regular study time, encourage your child to review words in their proper context as they relate to the chapter themes. For example, when studying the chapter about community places, Capítulo 3B, have your child bring flash cards for place names on a trip into town and review words for the places you pass along the way. Similarly, while studying Capítulo 4A vocabulary, bring out family photos and remind your child of the toys he or she used to have and the activities that he or she liked. Ask your child to name the toys and activities in Spanish. If your child can include multiple senses while studying (see the school and say *escuela,* or taste ice cream and say *helado*), it will help reinforce study and will aid in vocabulary retention.
- Motivate your child with praise for small jobs well done, not just for big exams and final grades. A memorized vocabulary list is something to be proud of!

*Review:*

- Encourage your child to review previously learned material frequently, and not just before a test. Remember, learning a language is a building process, and it is important to keep using what you've already learned.
- To aid vocabulary memorization, suggest that your child try several different methods, such as saying words aloud while looking at a picture of the items, writing the words, acting them out while saying them, and so on.
- Suggest that your child organize new material using charts, graphs, pictures with labels, or other visuals that can be posted in the study area. A daily review of those visuals will help keep the material fresh.
- Help your child drill new vocabulary and grammar by using the charts and lists in the **textbook.**

*Resources:*

- Offer to help frequently! Your child may have great ideas for how you can facilitate his or her learning experience.
- Ask your child's teacher, or encourage your child to ask, about how to best prepare for and what to expect on tests and quizzes.
- Ask your child's teacher about access to the eText and the digital course on Pearson Realize. These digital tools provide access to audio recordings and videos that support the text. The more your child sees and hears the language, the greater the retention.

Above all, help your child understand that a language is not acquired overnight. Just as for a first language, there is a gradual process for learning a second one. It takes time and patience, and it is important to know that mistakes are a completely natural part of the process. Remind your child that it took years to become proficient in his or her first language, and that the second one will also take time. Praise your child for even small progress in the ability to communicate in Spanish, and provide opportunities for your child to hear and use the language.

Don't hesitate to ask your child's teacher for ideas. You will find the teacher eager to help you. You may also be able to help the teacher understand special needs that your child may have, and work together with him or her to find the best techniques for helping your child learn.

Learning to speak another language is one of the most gratifying experiences a person can have. We know that your child will benefit from the effort, and will acquire a skill that will serve to enrich his or her life.

Copy the word or phrase in the space provided. Be sure to include the article for each noun.

| | | |
|---|---|---|
| **¿Quién(es)?** | **¿Cómo?** | **¿De dónde?** |
| _____ | _____ | _____ |
| **viejo, vieja** | **atrevido, atrevida** | **desordenado, desordenada** |
| _____ _____ | _____ _____ | _____ _____ |
| **reservado, reservada** | **gracioso, graciosa** | **sociable** |
| _____ _____ | _____ _____ | _____ _____ |

These blank cards can be used to write and practice other Spanish vocabulary for the chapter.

_____  _____  _____

_____  _____  _____

_____  _____  _____

**Para empezar**    Fecha _____    **Vocabulary Check, Sheet 1**

Tear out this page. Write the English words on the lines. Fold the paper along the dotted line to see the correct answers so you can check your work.

¿Cómo eres tú?                 _____

alto, alta                          _____

atrevido, atrevida             _____

bajo, baja                         _____

desordenado,                    _____
desordenada

estudioso,                         _____
estudiosa

gracioso, graciosa            _____

guapo, guapa                   _____

impaciente                        _____

inteligente                        _____

ordenado,                         _____
ordenada

reservado,                        _____
reservada

sociable                           _____

trabajador,                       _____
trabajadora

Fold In

Tear out this page. Write the Spanish words on the lines. Fold the paper along the dotted line to see the correct answers so you can check your work.

What are you like? _____

tall _____

daring _____

short _____

messy _____

studious _____

funny _____

good-looking _____

impatient _____

intelligent _____

neat _____

reserved, shy _____

sociable _____

hard-working _____

Fold In

## Adjectives (p. 3)

- Remember that adjectives describe nouns: people, places, and things. The following is a list of some common adjectives in Spanish.

| Masculine | | Feminine | |
|---|---|---|---|
| **Singular** | **Plural** | **Singular** | **Plural** |
| serio | serios | seria | serias |
| deportista | deportistas | deportista | deportistas |
| trabajador | trabajadores | trabajadora | trabajadoras |
| paciente | pacientes | paciente | pacientes |
| joven | jóvenes | joven | jóvenes |

**A.** Read each sentence. Circle the adjective and underline the noun. Follow the model.

**Modelo**   Enrique es un <u>joven</u> (serio.)

1. Mi primo es joven.

2. Mis hermanas son chicas jóvenes.

3. Carlos y Pedro son chicos deportistas.

4. Tú eres una persona paciente.

5. Yo soy una chica trabajadora.

6. Nosotras somos estudiantes serias.

- In Spanish, if a person, place, or thing is masculine, the adjective that describes it must be masculine: **El *chico* es muy *serio*.**
- If it's feminine, then the adjective must be feminine: ***María* es muy *alta*.**

**B.** Find the noun in each sentence below. Determine whether each noun is masculine or feminine and write **M** for masculine and **F** for feminine in the first blank. Then, fill in the missing letter in each adjective: **-o** for masculine nouns and **-a** for feminine nouns. Follow the model.

**Modelo**   _M_ Ricardo es muy seri_o_.

1. ___ Mi amiga Karla es alt___.

2. ___ Mi tía es una mujer ordenad___.

3. ___ Mi abuelo es un hombre desordenad___.

4. ___ Ese chico es muy gracios___.

## Adjectives (*continued*)

- In Spanish, if the person, place, or thing is singular, the adjective that describes it must be singular.
  **Mi hermano es paciente.** *My brother is patient.*
- If the person, place, or thing is plural, then the adjective is also plural.
  **Mis abuelos son pacientes.** *My grandparents are patient.*

**C.** Circle the adjective that best completes the sentence. Use the underlined word to help you. Follow the model.

| Modelo | Mi <u>abuela</u> es | **a.** graciosa. | **b.** graciosas. |
|--------|---------------------|------------------|-------------------|

**1.** Mis <u>hermanas</u> son       **a.** joven.          **b.** jóvenes.

**2.** <u>Pedro</u> es              **a.** guapo.          **b.** guapos.

**3.** Los <u>niños</u> son         **a.** serios.         **b.** serio.

**4.** <u>Marta</u> es              **a.** trabajadoras.   **b.** trabajadora.

**5.** <u>Eduardo</u> es            **a.** altos.          **b.** alto.

**6.** <u>Nosotras</u> somos        **a.** desordenadas.   **b.** desordenada.

**D.** Look at each sentence below and write the correct ending in the space provided. Follow the model.

| Modelo | María y Anita son chicas muy simpátic_**as**_. |
|--------|-----------------------------------------------|

**1.** Tú no eres una chica ordenad_____.

**2.** Mis primos son chicos gracios_____.

**3.** Nosotros somos personas estudios_____.

**4.** Tú y Pancho son estudiantes reservad_____.

**5.** Mi padre es un hombre baj_____.

**6.** Mis hermanos no son niños atrevid_____.

**7.** Nacho es un chico sociabl_____.

**Para empezar**    Fecha _____

# The verb *ser* (p. 5)

- **Ser** is an irregular verb and it means "to be." These are its present-tense forms:

| yo | **soy** | I am | nosotros(as) | **somos** | We are |
|----|---------|------|--------------|-----------|--------|
| tú | **eres** | You are (*fam.*) | vosotros(as) | **sois** | You are (*fam., pl.*) |
| Ud./él/ella | **es** | He, she is; You are (*form.*) | Uds./ellos/ellas | **son** | They are; You are (*form.*) |

- Remember that you can use **ser** with adjectives to tell what someone is like:

  **Esas chicas son altas.** *Those girls are tall.*

**A.** Choose the correct form of the verb **ser** in the word bank to complete the sentences. Follow the model.

| eres | somos | soy | son | es |
|------|-------|-----|-----|-----|

**Modelo**   Tú ____*eres*____ reservado.

**1.** Yo _____ sociable.

**2.** Nosotros _____ deportistas.

**3.** Elena _____ alta.

**4.** Tú _____ inteligente.

**5.** Ustedes _____ trabajadores.

- To tell where someone is from, use **ser + de +** place:

  **Ricardo es de México.** *Ricardo is from Mexico.*

**B.** Say where each of the people is from below based on their nationality. Follow the model.

**Modelo**   Linda: venezolana   ___*Linda*___ ___*es*___ ___*de*___ Venezuela.

**1.** Juan Carlos y Sofía: españoles  _____ _____ _____ España.

**2.** Rosa: guatemalteca  _____ _____ _____ Guatemala.

**3.** tú: mexicano  _____ _____ _____ México.

**4.** Orlando: cubano  _____ _____ _____ Cuba.

**5.** Luz y Marisol: colombianas  _____ _____ _____ Colombia.

**6.** Mercedes y yo: panameñas  _____ _____ _____ Panamá.

Nombre _____   Hora _____

Fecha _____   **Vocabulary Flash Cards, Sheet 3**

Copy the word or phrase in the space provided. Be sure to include the article for each noun.

| | | |
|---|---|---|
| **bailar** <br><br><br> _____ | **cantar** <br><br><br> _____ | **caminar** <br><br><br> _____ |
| **comer** <br><br><br> _____ | **correr** <br><br><br> _____ | **dibujar** <br><br><br> _____ |
| **escuchar música** <br><br><br> _____ <br><br> _____ | **usar la computadora** <br><br><br> _____ <br><br> _____ | **practicar deportes** <br><br><br> _____ <br><br> _____ |

**Para empezar**   Fecha _____   **Vocabulary Check, Sheet 3**

Tear out this page. Write the English words on the lines. Fold the paper along the dotted line to see the correct answers so you can check your work.

practicar deportes   _____

bailar   _____

caminar   _____

cantar   _____

comer   _____

dibujar   _____

nadar   _____

usar la computadora   _____

música   _____

a menudo   _____

a veces   _____

nunca   _____

siempre   _____

después (de)   _____

Fold In →

## Para empezar

Tear out this page. Write the Spanish words on the lines. Fold the paper along the dotted line to see the correct answers so you can check your work.

to play sports        _____

to dance              _____

to walk               _____

to sing               _____

to eat                _____

to draw               _____

to swim               _____

to use the computer   _____

music                 _____

often                 _____

sometimes             _____

never                 _____

always                _____

afterwards, after     _____

Fold In ↓

## Present tense of regular verbs (p. 9)

- **Hablar** (*to talk*), **comer** (*to eat*), and **vivir** (*to live*) are regular verbs. To form the present tense, drop the **-ar, -er,** or **-ir** endings and add the present-tense endings.

|  | *hablar* | *comer* | *vivir* |
|---|---|---|---|
| yo | **hablo** | **como** | **vivo** |
| tú | **hablas** | **comes** | **vives** |
| usted/él/ella | **habla** | **come** | **vive** |
| nosotros/nosotras | **hablamos** | **comemos** | **vivimos** |
| vosotros/vosotras | **habláis** | **coméis** | **vivís** |
| ustedes/ellos/ellas | **hablan** | **comen** | **viven** |

**A.** Circle the present-tense verb form in each sentence.

**Modelo**   Nosotros (corremos) en el parque.

1. Mis amigas viven en Nueva York.

2. Carlos come en casa a las seis.

3. Yo escribo mi tarea en el cuaderno.

4. Ustedes hablan inglés y español.

**B.** Look at the drawings below. Complete each description by circling the correct form of the verb using the subject pronouns given.

**Modelo**   Él ( **escuchan** / (**escucha**) ) la radio.

1.   Andrea ( **escribimos** / **escribe** ) cuentos.

2.   Tú ( **usa** / **usas** ) la computadora.   ⟶

# Present tense of regular verbs (*continued*)

3. Nosotras ( **comes** / **comemos** ).

4. Marta ( **toca** / **tocamos** ) la guitarra.

5. Ustedes ( **cantan** / **canto** ) muy bien.

**C.** Choose the correct ending for each incomplete verb and draw a line beneath your choice. Follow the model.

**Modelo**   Ana camin( **-a** / **-e** ) a la escuela.

1. Tomás escrib( **-a** / **-e** ) cuentos fantásticos.

2. Nosotros practic( **-amos** / **-emos** ) muchos deportes.

3. Yo escuch( **-a** / **-o** ) la música clásica.

4. Juan y Lola le( **-en** / **-an** ) novelas de horror.

**D.** Write the correct form of each verb in the space provided.

**Modelo**   Luis _____*nada*_____ (**nadar**) en la piscina.

1. Lolis _____ (**correr**) en el parque todos los días.

2. ¿Tú _____ (**montar**) en monopatín?

3. Vicente y yo _____ (**comer**) en el restaurante mexicano.

4. Tú y Rodrigo _____ (**vivir**) en el mismo pueblo.

5. Yo _____ (**sacar**) la basura.

## Presentación escrita (p. 13)

**Task:** Write a poem in the shape of a diamond. The poem is going to describe you.

**A.** Look at the poem Linda has written about herself. Circle all the words she uses to say what she is or is not like (adjectives). Then, underline all the words that tell what Linda does or does not do (verbs). The first ones have been done for you.

Me llamo Linda.

No soy ni seria ni vieja.

Soy alta, sociable, estudiosa.

Todos los días yo escucho música, leo, corro, uso la computadora.

En el verano mis amigos y yo nadamos, cantamos, bailamos.

Nunca patino ni monto en bicicleta.

¡Así soy yo!

**B.** Look at the word list below and complete the sentence with two words from the list that do *not* describe you. Remember to use the **-o** ending if you are a boy and **-a** if you are a girl. And remember that **sociable** and **impaciente** don't change gender. Follow the model.

| alto, -a | atrevido, -a | desordenado, -a | estudioso, -a | gracioso, -a |
|----------|--------------|-----------------|---------------|--------------|
| ordenado, -a | reservado, -a | sociable | impaciente | |

**Modelo**   No soy ni _ordenada_ ni _sociable_.

No soy ni _____ ni _____.

**C.** Now, choose three words from the list in **part A** that describe you. Complete the sentence with those words. Be sure to use the appropriate endings on words you choose.

Soy _____, _____ y _____.

**Para empezar**

Fecha _____

# Presentación escrita (*continued*)

**D.** Circle the activities in the box that you like to do and complete the sentence below with those activities.

| | | | |
|---|---|---|---|
| bailo | canto | camino | dibujo |
| leo revistas | monto en bicicleta | uso la computadora | escucho música |

Todos los días yo _____, _____, _____ y

_____.

**E.** Which of the activities in **part D** do you like to do with friends? Complete the sentence below using three of those activities.

En el verano, mis amigos y yo _____, _____ y

_____.

**F.** Complete the sentence below with two activities you never do.

Nunca _____ ni _____.

**G.** Finally, use your answers from **parts B** through **F** to complete this poem in the shape of a diamond.

Me llamo _____.

No soy ni _____ ni _____.

Soy _____, _____ y _____.

Todos los días yo _____, _____,

_____ y _____.

Mis amigos y yo _____, _____ y _____.

Nunca _____ ni _____.

¡Así soy yo!

# The verb *tener* (p. 15)

- Remember that **tener** means "to have." It is also used to tell how old you are (**tener años**), or to say that you're hungry (**tener hambre**), sleepy (**tener sueño**), or thirsty (**tener sed**).

- Here are the present-tense forms of **tener**:

| yo | tengo | nosotros/nosotras | tenemos |
|---|---|---|---|
| tú | tienes | vosotros/vosotras | tenéis |
| usted/él/ella | tiene | ustedes/ellos/ellas | tienen |

**A.** Circle the correct form of **tener** to complete each sentence.

**Modelo**    Alicia (( tiene )/ tenemos ) un reloj nuevo.

1. Yo no ( tienes / **tengo** ) los carteles.

2. Paco y Lulú ( tenemos / **tienen** ) hambre.

3. Nosotros ( **tenemos** / tienen ) los bolígrafos.

4. Marco ( **tiene** / tienes ) 14 años.

5. ¿Cuántos diccionarios ( tiene / **tienes** ) tú?

6. Alicia y tú no ( **tienen** / tienes ) calculadoras, ¿verdad?

- To say that someone has to do something, use **tener** + **que** + infinitive.
  **Marta tiene que estudiar.** *Marta has to study.*

**B.** Write the correct form of **tener** + **que** to tell what these people have to do.

**Modelo**    Susana ____*tiene*____ ____*que*____ esquiar.

1. Yo _____ _____ practicar deportes.

2. Nosotros _____ _____ comer a las 6.

3. Juana y Julio _____ _____ ir a clase.

4. Los estudiantes _____ _____ hacer la tarea.

5. Tú _____ _____ traer el libro a clase.

# Verbs with irregular *yo* forms

- The **yo** form of **tener** in the present tense is irregular. It ends in **-go (Yo tengo)**.
- Other verbs that are irregular in the **yo** form are:

| hacer (to do, to make) | poner (to put) | traer (to bring) |
|---|---|---|
| hago | pongo | traigo |

**C.** Write the **yo** form of each verb in parentheses.

1. Yo (**tener**) ___ un asiento.
2. Yo (**poner**) ___ los cuadernos en la mesa.
3. Yo (**hacer**) ___ la tarea.
4. Yo (**traer**) ___ la papelera.

**D.** Complete the sentences with forms of **traer, tener, poner,** or **hacer.** Follow the model.

**Modelo** (**traer**) Alejandro ___*trae*___ su mochila a clase.

1. (**tener**) Raúl y yo ___ que estudiar.
2. (**hacer**) Yo ___ la tarea.
3. (**poner**) Juliana ___ sus libros en su mochila.
4. (**hacer**) Tú ___ un experimento en la clase de ciencias naturales.
5. (**traer**) Los estudiantes no ___ un sacapuntas a clase.
6. (**poner**) Yo ___ una manzana en el escritorio del profesor.

Nombre _____          Hora _____

**Capítulo 1A**     Fecha _____     **Vocabulary Flash Cards, Sheet 1**

Write the Spanish vocabulary word or phrase below each picture. Be sure to include the article for each noun.

_____

_____

_____

_____

_____

_____

_____

_____

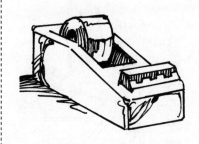

_____

_____

_____

_____

_____  _____

_____

_____

_____

_____

_____

*Guided Practice Activities* ▬ *Vocabulary Flash Cards 1A*  **17**

**Capítulo 1A**    Fecha _____    **Vocabulary Flash Cards, Sheet 2**

Write the Spanish vocabulary word or phrase below each picture. Be sure to include the article for each noun.

_____

_____

_____

_____

_____

_____

_____

_____

_____

_____

_____

_____

_____

_____

_____

_____

_____

_____

Write the Spanish vocabulary word below each picture. If there is a word or phrase, copy it in the space provided. Be sure to include the article for each noun.

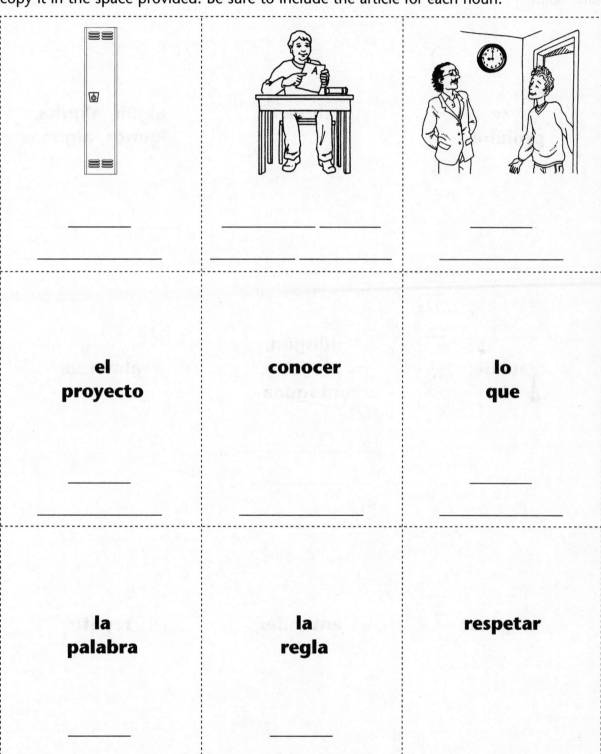

| | | |
|---|---|---|
| _____ _____ | _____ _____ | _____ _____ |
| **el proyecto** | **conocer** | **lo que** |
| _____ _____ | _____ _____ | _____ _____ |
| **la palabra** | **la regla** | **respetar** |
| _____ _____ | _____ _____ | _____ _____ |

Copy the word or phrase in the space provided. Be sure to include the article for each noun.

| | | |
|---|---|---|
| **se prohíbe...** <br><br> _____ <br> _____ | **alguien** <br><br> _____ <br> _____ | **algún, alguna, algunos, algunas** <br><br> _____ _____ <br> _____ _____ |
| **nadie** <br><br> _____ | **ningún, ninguno, ninguna** <br><br> _____ <br> _____ | **almorzar** <br><br> _____ |
| **empezar** <br><br> _____ | **entender** <br><br> _____ | **repetir** <br><br> _____ |

Copy the word or phrase in the space provided. These blank cards can be used to write and practice other Spanish vocabulary for the chapter.

**sobre**

_____        _____        _____

_____        _____        _____

_____        _____        _____

These blank cards can be used to write and practice other Spanish vocabulary for the chapter.

Tear out this page. Write the English words on the lines. Fold the paper along the dotted line to see the correct answers so you can check your work.

prestar atención  _____

se prohíbe...  _____

la regla  _____

respetar  _____

entregar  _____

explicar  _____

pedir ayuda  _____

el informe  _____

el proyecto  _____

alguien  _____

nadie  _____

contestar  _____

discutir  _____

hacer una pregunta  _____

llegar tarde  _____

Fold In

Tear out this page. Write the Spanish words on the lines. Fold the paper along the dotted line to see the correct answers so you can check your work.

to pay attention          _____

it's forbidden...          _____

rule          _____

to respect          _____

to turn in          _____

to explain          _____

to ask for help          _____

report          _____

project          _____

someone, anyone          _____

no one, nobody          _____

to answer          _____

to discuss          _____

to ask a question          _____

to arrive late          _____

Fold In

Tear out this page. Write the English words on the lines. Fold the paper along the dotted line to see the correct answers so you can check your work.

aprender de memoria    _____

el laboratorio    _____

la palabra    _____

sacar una buena nota    _____

a tiempo    _____

el armario    _____

el asiento    _____

el carnet de identidad    _____

la cinta adhesiva    _____

la grapadora    _____

los materiales    _____

las tijeras    _____

Fold In →

Tear out this page. Write the Spanish words on the lines. Fold the paper along the dotted line to see the correct answers so you can check your work.

to memorize _____

laboratory _____

word _____

to get a good
grade _____

on time _____

locker _____

seat _____

I.D. card _____

transparent tape _____

stapler _____

supplies, materials _____

scissors _____

Fold In

# Stem-changing verbs (p. 27)

- Stem-changing verbs have one spelling change in their stem in the present tense:
  alm**o**rzar → Yo alm**ue**rzo en la escuela.
- The stem change, as seen in the verb chart below, resembles a shoe because the
  **nosotros(as)** and **vosotros(as)** forms do not change.

| yo | **duermo** | nosotros/ nosotras | **dormimos** |
|---|---|---|---|
| tú | **duermes** | vosotros/ vosotras | **dormís** |
| usted/él/ella | **duerme** | ustedes/ellos/ellas | **duermen** |

- Look at the **yo** form of the verbs in the chart below.

| e → ie | o → ue | e → i | u → ue |
|---|---|---|---|
| empezar → emp**ie**zo | poder → p**ue**do | pedir → p**i**do | jugar → j**ue**go |
| entender → ent**ie**ndo | almorzar → alm**ue**rzo | repetir → rep**i**to | |
| | | servir → s**i**rvo | |

**A.** Look at the verbs below and connect the letter in each stem with the letters it changes to in the conjugated form. Follow the model.

**Modelo**  empezar ⌒→ empiezo

1. poder       puede
2. pedir       pides
3. servir      sirven

4. almorzar    almuerzo
5. jugar       juega
6. entender    entienden

**B.** Fill in the blanks with the correct stem-change letters for each verb in the sentences below. Follow the model.

**Modelo**  Miguel alm_u_ _e_rza en la cafetería.

1. Los chicos j____ ____gan al fútbol americano.
2. El camarero s_____rve la comida a tiempo.
3. Yo p_____do café con leche en el bar.
4. La clase emp____ ____za a las cuatro y media.
5. La manzana c____ ____sta veinticinco centavos.
6. Los estudiantes rep_____ten lo que dice la profesora.

# Stem-changing verbs (*continued*)

- Remember that the **nosotros** and **vosotros** forms do not change their stem.

**C.** Look at each pair of sentences below. In the space provided in the second sentence, write the **nosotros** form of the underlined verb from the first sentence to say that we don't do what the persons in the first sentence do. Follow the model.

Modelo    Claudia empieza a hablar. Nosotros no ___*empezamos*___ a hablar.

1. Tú juegas al fútbol. Nosotros no _____ al fútbol.

2. Jorge entiende la clase. Nosotros no _____ la clase.

3. Yo almuerzo con Juan y Rebeca. Nosotros no _____ con Juan y Rebeca.

4. Rebeca pide una cinta adhesiva y una grapadora.

   Nosotros no _____ una cinta adhesiva y una grapadora.

**D.** Answer the following questions choosing the stem-changing verb that makes the most sense in the sentence. Once you have chosen a verb, write the correct form in the space provided. Follow the model.

Modelo    Es el mediodía y tú tienes hambre. ¿Qué haces tú?
          Yo _____*almuerzo*_____ ( almorzar / entender ) en la cafetería.

1. Son las diez de la noche y nosotras estamos cansadas. ¿Qué hacemos?

   Nosotras _____ ( querer / dormir ).

2. Juan y Felipe son camareros en un restaurante. ¿Qué hacen todos los días?

   Ellos _____ ( repetir / servir ) la comida.

3. Tú sacas buenas notas en la clase de ciencias naturales. ¿Por qué?

   Porque yo _____ ( entender / dormir ) la información.

4. Nosotros estamos en el equipo de voléibol. ¿Qué hacemos?

   Nosotros _____ ( jugar / almorzar ) al voléibol.

# Affirmative and negative words (p. 31)

- Affirmative and negative words are opposites.
- Affirmative words are used to say that something does exist, or that it does happen. Negative words are used to say that something doesn't exist, or that it doesn't happen.
- **Yo siempre hago preguntas** is an affirmative sentence. It means "I always ask questions."
- **Yo nunca hago preguntas** is a negative sentence. It means "I never ask questions."

| Affirmative | Negative |
|---|---|
| **alguien**  *someone, anyone* | **nadie**  *no one, nobody* |
| **algo**  *something* | **nada**  *nothing* |
| **algún**  *some, any*<br>⌈ **alguno(s)** ⌉<br>⌊ **alguna(s)** ⌋ | **ningún**  *no, none, not any*<br>⌈ **ninguno** ⌉<br>⌊ **ninguna** ⌋ |
| **siempre**  *always* | **nunca**  *never* |
| **también**  *also, too* | **tampoco**  *neither, either* |

**A.** Rubén and Nora are talking about a class. Look at the underlined affirmative or negative words in each sentence. Then, write + next to the sentence if the word is affirmative and − if the word is negative. The first one is done for you.

1. RUBÉN:  ¿Por qué tú <u>siempre</u> haces preguntas en esa clase? _____

   NORA:  Porque yo <u>nunca</u> entiendo y me gusta entender. _____

2. RUBÉN:  ¿Conoces a Marina? A ella <u>también</u> le gusta hacer preguntas. _____

   NORA:  ¡Sí! Ella <u>tampoco</u> entiende la clase. _____

3. RUBÉN:  Yo <u>siempre</u> te quiero ayudar. _____

   NORA:  Yo <u>también</u> quiero ayudar a Marina. _____

**B.** Each sentence below has an affirmative or negative word from the above chart. Find the word and circle it. Then, write its opposite in the blank. Follow the model.

Modelo   Yo (siempre) respeto las reglas.     *nunca*

1. Alguien contesta la pregunta.     _____

2. Lucía siempre llega tarde.     _____

3. Mis padres nunca dan un discurso.     _____

# Affirmative and negative words (*continued*)

4. Tú también haces tu proyecto. _____

5. Marta y María tampoco piden ayuda. _____

6. Yo no tengo ninguna clase aburrida. _____

- When you want to say "some," change the ending of **alguno** so it matches what you're describing in gender (masculine or feminine) and number (singular or plural): **alguna chica, algunos libros, algunas chicas.** The same is true for **ninguno: ninguna clase.**

- Before a masculine singular noun, **alguno** and **ninguno** change to **algún** and **ningún.**

**C.** Look at the list of school supplies below. Is the word (or words) masculine or feminine, singular or plural? Circle the correct form of **alguno** or **ninguno** in parentheses.

1. ( algunas / algunos ) asientos

2. ( alguna / algunos ) cinta adhesiva

3. ( algunos / algún ) armario

4. ( ningún / ninguna ) libro

5. ( algunos / alguna ) materiales

6. ( ninguna / ningún ) grapadora

**D.** Circle the letter of the answer that best completes each sentence.

1. —¿Conoces a alguien en el laboratorio?
   —No, yo no conozco a
   **a.** alguien.          **b.** nadie.

2. —¿Va a comer algo Anita?
   —No, no va a comer
   **a.** algo.          **b.** nada.

3. —¿Conoce Sandra a alguien en el laboratorio?
   —Sí, ella conoce a
   **a.** alguien.          **b.** nadie.

4. —¿Conoce el maestro a alguien en el laboratorio?
   —No, el maestro no conoce a
   **a.** alguien.          **b.** nadie.

5. —¿Alfonso siempre llega a clase a tiempo?
   —Sí, él ___ llega a tiempo.
   **a.** siempre          **b.** nunca

# Lectura: Seis pasos para estudiar mejor... (pp. 34–35)

**A.** The reading in your textbook is an article about good study habits. First, look at the heads and subheads in the article. They can help you understand what the material will be about before you begin reading. Then, based on the information you read in the heads and subheads, list three things you would expect to find in this article.

1. _____

2. _____

3. _____

**B.** The following words are cognates from the reading. Remember that cognates are words that have similar spellings and meanings in English and Spanish. Write the letter of the English word that matches the Spanish word.

1. ____ comprender     **a.** comprehend     **b.** communicate

2. ____ clases     **a.** cases     **b.** classes

3. ____ atención     **a.** attitude     **b.** attention

4. ____ hábitos     **a.** habits     **b.** abilities

**C.** Read the following excerpt from the first section of the article in your textbook. Then, choose the best option to complete the sentences below based on the excerpt. Write the answers in the space provided. The first one has been done for you.

> *Presta atención: los buenos hábitos de estudio empiezan en la clase*
>
> *¿Te cuesta prestar atención en clase? ¿Te sientas cerca de una persona que habla mucho o es muy ruidosa? ¿No ves bien la pizarra? Asegúrate de sentarte en un buen sitio para poder prestar atención. Si hay algo que te impide prestar atención o tomar buenos apuntes en clase, coméntaselo al profesor o a tus padres.*

1. Los buenos hábitos de estudio empiezan ___*en la clase*.___
   **a.** en la biblioteca     **b.** en la clase     **c.** en la calle

2. El artículo pregunta si el estudiante _____.
   **a.** hace sus tareas     **b.** tiene hambre     **c.** ve bien la pizarra

3. El estudiante debe _____ para poder prestar atención.
   **a.** sentarse en un buen sitio     **b.** usar la tableta     **c.** mirar el libro

4. Si el estudiante no puede tomar buenos apuntes, debe _____.
   **a.** usar otro lápiz     **b.** decírselo al profesor o a sus padres     **c.** pedir ayuda a un amigo

**Capítulo 1A**

# Presentación oral (p. 37)

**Task:** You have been invited to be a school principal for a day. As principal, you will make new school rules and display them on a poster. Then, you will present your poster to a partner.

**A.** Think about what students will and will not be allowed to do in your school. Then list some phrases to describe these rules. A few phrases have been provided to get you started.

llegar a tiempo, hacer la tarea, conocer al director, _____,

_____, _____, _____

**B.** Using the phrases from **part A**, complete the columns. In the **Hay que...** column, write three phrases to describe what students should do at your school. In the **Se prohíbe...** column, write three phrases to describe what should not be done at your school. One has been done for you.

| *Hay que...* | *Se prohíbe...* |
| --- | --- |
| 1. _hacer la tarea_ | 1. _____ |
| 2. _____ | 2. _____ |
| 3. _____ | 3. _____ |

**C.** On a piece of posterboard, write out *complete* sentences using your answers from **part B**. Leave space between each for your drawings. Follow the models.

Modelos   Hay que _____ _hacer la tarea_ _____ .

Se prohíbe _llegar tarde a la clase_ _____ .

**D.** Now, illustrate each of your school rules on the poster.

**E.** Tell a partner about your school rules. Refer to the illustrations on your poster as you speak. Be sure to:

• include three things that students are allowed and three things that are not allowed

• use complete sentences

• speak clearly

# The verb *ir* (p. 43)

- The verb **ir** is used to say where someone goes or is going.
  **Voy a casa.**      *I'm going home.*
  **Vamos al café.**      *We're going to the café.*
- Look at the forms of **ir** below:

| yo | **voy** | nosotros/nosotras | **vamos** |
|---|---|---|---|
| tú | **vas** | vosotros/vosotras | **vais** |
| usted/él/ella | **va** | ustedes/ellos/ellas | **van** |

**A.** Circle the correct form of the verb **ir** in each sentence. Follow the model.

**Modelo**    Amalia ( voy / (va) ) al gimnasio.

1. ¡Nosotros ( van / vamos ) al parque!

2. ¿A qué hora ( vas / voy ) tú a la biblioteca?

3. Mis padres ( van / vas ) a la piscina.

4. Yo ( voy / van ) al trabajo.

5. ¿Cuándo ( voy / va ) la familia al restaurante mexicano?

- To tell what someone is going to do, use **ir** + **a** + infinitive.
  **Voy a ver una película.**      *I'm going to see a movie.*
  **Vamos a estudiar esta tarde.**      *We are going to study this afternoon.*

**B.** Write the correct form of **ir** + **a** to tell what these people are going to do. Follow the model.

**Modelo**    Jorge ____*va*____ ___*a*___ salir.

1. Ellas _____ _____ estudiar.

2. Yo _____ _____ leer.

3. Marta _____ _____ nadar.

4. Tulio y Ana _____ _____ comer en un restaurante.

5. Chucho y yo _____ _____ comer.

Write the Spanish vocabulary word or phrase below each picture. Be sure to include the article for each noun.

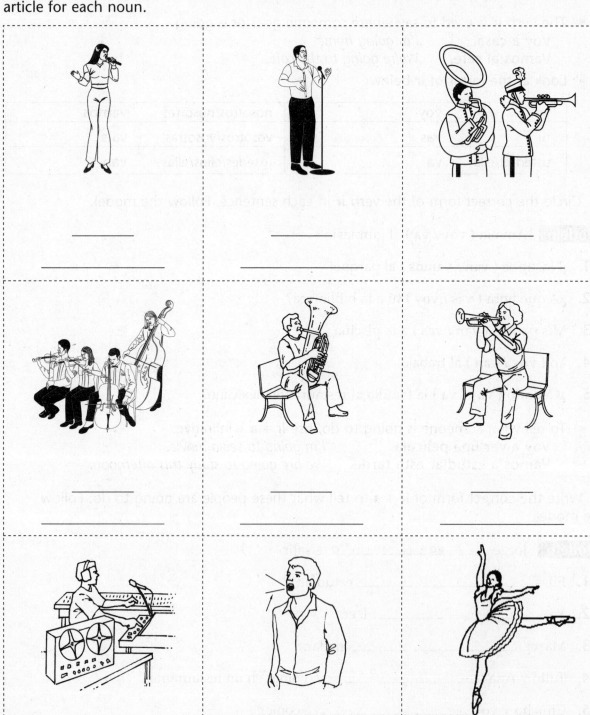

Nombre _____     Hora _____

### Capítulo 1B

Fecha _____     **Vocabulary Flash Cards, Sheet 2**

Write the Spanish vocabulary word or phrase below each picture. Be sure to include the article for each noun.

_____

_____

_____

_____

_____

_____

_____

_____

_____

_____

_____

_____

_____

_____

_____

_____

_____

_____

Write the Spanish vocabulary word or phrase below each picture. Be sure to include the article for each noun.

_____

_____

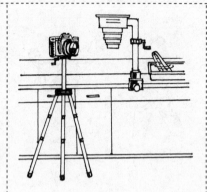

_____

_____

_____

_____

_____

_____

_____

_____

_____

_____

_____

_____

_____

_____

_____

_____

Copy the word or phrase in the space provided. Be sure to include the article for each noun.

| | | |
|---|---|---|
| **la canción** | **las actividades extracurriculares** | **navegar en la Red** |
| **el club** | **el club atlético** | **el equipo** |
| **ser miembro** | **el pasatiempo** | **la reunión** |

Copy the word or phrase in the space provided. Be sure to include the article for each noun.

| | | |
|---|---|---|
| **el coro** <br><br> _____ <br> _____ | **ensayar** <br><br> _____ | **el ensayo** <br><br> _____ <br> _____ |
| **asistir a** <br><br> _____ <br> _____ | **ganar** <br><br> _____ | **participar (en)** <br><br> _____ _____ |
| **tomar lecciones** <br><br> _____ <br> _____ | **volver** <br><br> _____ | **entre** <br><br> _____ |

Copy the word or phrase in the space provided. Be sure to include the article for each noun.

| | | |
|---|---|---|
| **el interés** | **la oportunidad** | **¿Cuánto tiempo hace que...?** |
| _____ <br> _____ | _____ <br> _____ | _____ _____ <br> _____ |
| **saber** | **conocer** | **el miembro** |
| _____ | _____ | _____ <br> _____ |
| **Hace + *time* + que...** | **tantos, tantas + *noun* + como** | **tan + *adj.* + como** |
| _____ _____ <br> _____ | _____ , _____ _____ | _____ _____ _____ <br> _____ |

These blank cards can be used to write and practice other Spanish vocabulary for the chapter.

_____     _____     _____

_____     _____     _____

_____     _____     _____

Tear out this page. Write the English words on the lines. Fold the paper along the dotted line to see the correct answers so you can check your work.

el músico, la música _____

la orquesta _____

el equipo _____

la natación _____

el ajedrez _____

la fotografía _____

hacer una búsqueda _____

ser miembro _____

ganar _____

el pasatiempo _____

participar (en) _____

la reunión _____

volver _____

asistir a _____

Fold In

Tear out this page. Write the Spanish words on the lines. Fold the paper along the dotted line to see the correct answers so you can check your work.

musician              _____

orchestra             _____

team                  _____

swimming              _____

chess                 _____

photography           _____

to do a search        _____

to be a member        _____

to win, to earn       _____

pastime               _____

to participate (in)   _____

meeting               _____

to return             _____

to attend             _____

Fold In

Tear out this page. Write the English words on the lines. Fold the paper along the dotted line to see the correct answers so you can check your work.

el hockey _____

jugar a los bolos _____

hacer gimnasia _____

las artes marciales _____

el animador,
la animadora _____

la práctica _____

los jóvenes _____

el club _____

la banda _____

el bailarín,
la bailarina _____

el coro _____

ensayar _____

tomar lecciones _____

entre _____

el interés _____

Fold In

Tear out this page. Write the Spanish words on the lines. Fold the paper along the dotted line to see the correct answers so you can check your work.

hockey                _____

to bowl               _____

to do gymnastics      _____

martial arts          _____

cheerleader           _____

practice              _____

young people          _____

club                  _____

band                  _____

dancer                _____

chorus, choir         _____

to rehearse           _____

to take lessons       _____

among, between        _____

interest              _____

Fold In

# Making comparisons (p. 53)

- To say that people or things are equal to each other, use **tan** + *adjective* + **como**.
  **El hockey es tan popular como la natación.**
  *Hockey is as popular as swimming.*
- To say that people or things are not equal, use the negative verb form.
  **El hockey no es tan popular como la natación.**
  *Hockey is not as popular as swimming.*

**A.** Fill in the blank with **tan**, **como**, or **es** to correctly complete the sentences. Follow the model.

**Modelo**   El hockey es tan popular ____*como*____ la fotografía.

1. La banda es _____ popular como la orquesta.

2. Jugar a los bolos no es tan popular _____ el ajedrez.

3. Hacer gimnasia _____ tan popular como las artes marciales.

4. Las animadoras no son _____ populares como los miembros del equipo.

5. El bailarín no es tan popular _____ el cantante.

**B.** Each person thinks the activities below are equal. Complete their thoughts by filling in the correct form of **ser**, the comparative expression **tan...como**, and the adjective in parentheses. Follow the model.

**Modelo**   Yo creo que cantar __*es*__ __*tan*__ __*divertido*__ __*como*__ (**divertido**) bailar.

1. Creo que el ajedrez ____ ____ _____ ____ (**interesante**) jugar a los bolos.

2. Yo creo que las dos actividades ____ ____ _____ ____ (**aburridas**) la fotografía.

3. Para mí el hockey ____ ____ _____ ____ (**emocionante**) bailar.

4. ¡Ay! Para mí, las actividades ____ ____ _____ ____ (**difíciles**) las clases de la escuela.

# Making comparisons (*continued*)

- Use **tanto, -a** + *noun* + **como** to say "as much as":
  **tanto interés como,** *as much interest as*
- Use **tantos, -as** + *noun* + **como** to say "as many as":
  **tantos jóvenes como,** *as many young people as*
- Note that **tanto** also agrees in gender and number with the item that is being compared.
  **Elena no hace tantas actividades extracurriculares como Juan.**
  *Elena doesn't do as many extracurricular activities as Juan.*

**C.** Look at the following sentences and decide if the underlined word is masculine or feminine, singular or plural. Then, circle the correct form of **tanto** in parentheses. Follow the model.

**Modelo**  Yo asisto a ( (tantas) / tanta ) <u>reuniones</u> como Elena.

1. Yo tengo ( **tantos** / **tantas** ) <u>prácticas</u> como mi hermano.

2. Juan toma ( **tantas** / **tanta** ) <u>lecciones</u> de artes marciales como Carlos.

3. Elena tiene ( **tantas** / **tantos** ) <u>pasatiempos</u> como Angélica.

4. Camilo tiene ( **tanto** / **tantos** ) <u>interés</u> en el hockey como Juan.

5. Hay ( **tantas** / **tantos** ) <u>bailarinas</u> como bailarines.

**D.** Write the correct form of **tanto (tanta/tantos/tantas)** in the following phrases. Remember that **tanto** agrees in gender and number with the noun. Follow the model.

**Modelo**  Hay _____*tantos*_____ chicos como chicas en el coro.

1. Hay _____ personas mayores como personas menores.

2. En la escuela hay _____ equipos de deportes como clubes.

3. Hay _____ profesores simpáticos como antipáticos.

4. Hago _____ trabajo como Javier.

5. La clase crea _____ páginas Web como los técnicos.

6. El hombre rico tiene _____ cuadros como un museo.

# The verbs *saber* and *conocer* (p. 56)

- These are the present tense forms of **saber** and **conocer**.

| yo | **sé** | nosotros/ nosotras | **sabemos** | yo | **conozco** | nosotros/ nosotras | **conocemos** |
|---|---|---|---|---|---|---|---|
| tú | **sabes** | vosotros/ vosotras | **sabéis** | tú | **conoces** | vosotros/ vosotras | **conocéis** |
| usted/ él/ella | **sabe** | ustedes/ ellos/ellas | **saben** | usted/ él/ella | **conoce** | ustedes/ ellos/ellas | **conocen** |

**A.** Circle the correct form of the verb **saber** or **conocer**.

1. Mi amiga ( **sabe** / **sabes** ) mucho del hockey.

2. Yo no ( **conoces** / **conozco** ) al cantante nuevo.

3. ¿Tú ( **conoces** / **conozco** ) a Juan?

4. ¿( **Sabemos** / **Saben** ) ustedes cuándo son las reuniones del club?

5. Mi madre y yo ( **conocemos** / **conocen** ) a un músico.

6. ¿( **Sabes** / **Sabemos** ) tú mi número de teléfono?

- **Saber** means to know information and facts.

   **¿Sabes si tenemos una reunión mañana?** *Do you know if we have a meeting tomorrow?*

- **Conocer** means to know a person or to be familiar with a place or thing. Use the **a** *personal* with **conocer** to say you know a person:

   **¿Conocen Uds. la música de Gloria Estefan?** *Do you know/Are you familiar with the music of Gloria Estefan?*

   **¿Conoces a María?** *Do you know María?*

**B.** Look at the following sentences. Decide if you would use the form of **conocer** or **saber** in parentheses. Circle your choice. Follow the model.

| | |
|---|---|
| **Modelo** Julián _____ la orquesta de San Francisco. | **a.** conoce  **b.** sabe |
| 1. ¿_____ tú el equipo profesional de fútbol en tu ciudad? | **a.** Sabes  **b.** Conoces |
| 2. La abuela _____ navegar en la Red. | **a.** sabe  **b.** conoce |
| 3. Nosotros _____ la ciudad de Boston. | **a.** sabemos  **b.** conocemos |
| 4. ¿_____ Uds. que el equipo ganó el partido? | **a.** Saben  **b.** Conocen |
| 5. Mis amigos y yo _____ jugar a los bolos. | **a.** conocemos  **b.** sabemos |

# The verbs *saber* and *conocer* (*continued*)

- Use the verb **saber** + *infinitive of another verb* to say that you know how to do something:

  **Sabemos hacer gimnasia.** *We know how to do gymnastics.*

**C.** Look at the pictures below. Complete the answers with the verb form of **saber** and the infinitive of another verb. Follow the model.

**Modelo** Kiko y Roberto saben patinar.

**1.** Andrés ____________ ____________ a los bolos.

**2.** Sara y Rebeca ____________ ____________ gimnasia.

**3.** Yo ____________ ____________ la guitarra.

**4.** ¿Tú no ____________ ____________ un disco?

**D.** Read the following sentences and decide whether **saber** or **conocer** should be used. Write an **S** for **saber** and a **C** for **conocer** in the first space. Then, write the form of the verb you chose to complete the sentence. The first one is done for you.

1. S Yo sé jugar a los bolos.
2. ____ Ellos no ________________ al profesor de música.
3. ____ Él no ________________ visitar salones de chat.
4. ____ Mis amigos y yo ________________ hacer una búsqueda en la Red.
5. ____ Nosotros no ________________ el club de ajedrez.

# *Hace* + time expressions (p. 58)

- When you want to ask how long something has been going on, you use ¿**Cuánto tiempo** + **hace que** + *present-tense verb*? For example,

  **¿Cuánto tiempo hace que eres miembro del coro?**
  *How long have you been a member of the choir?*

**A.** Look at the sentences using ¿**Cuánto tiempo** + **hace que...?** and write in the word that is missing from the sentence. Follow the model.

Modelo   ¿Cuánto tiempo hace _____*que*_____ ustedes ensayan con el club de música?

1. ¿Cuánto _____ hace que tú no asistes a las reuniones del club?

2. ¿Cuánto tiempo _____ que Juana toma lecciones de fotografía?

3. ¿Cuánto _____ hace que tus padres no vuelven a casa?

4. ¿_____ tiempo hace que nosotros no hacemos gimnasia?

5. ¿Cuánto tiempo hace _____ Paco no toca el saxofón?

- When you want to tell how long something has been going on, you use **hace** + *period of time* + **que** + *present-tense verb*. For example,

  **Hace cuatro meses que soy miembro del club atlético.**
  *I have been a member of the athletic team for four months.*

**B.** Complete the following answers using the present tense of the verb in parentheses. Follow the model.

Modelo   Hace tres días que nosotros _*ensayamos*_ (**ensayar**) con el club de música.

1. Hace un mes que ustedes no _____ (**volver**) al club atlético.

2. Hace dos años que Juana _____ (**tomar**) lecciones de fotografía.

3. Hace ocho semanas que tú no _____ (**asistir**) a las reuniones del club.

4. Hace cinco años que Elena y yo no _____ (**bailar**).

5. Hace diez meses que Tomás no _____ (**ir**) a Cancún.

# *Hace* + time expressions (*continued*)

**C.** Read the following questions and answer with the information provided in parentheses and the present tense of the verb. Follow the model.

Modelo   ¿Cuánto tiempo hace que tú participas en la natación? (dos meses)

Hace ___*dos*___ ___*meses*___ que yo ___*participo*___ en la natación.

1.  ¿Cuánto tiempo hace que Carlos juega en el equipo? (un año)

    Hace _____ _____ que Carlos _____ en el equipo.

2.  ¿Cuánto tiempo hace que ustedes navegan en la Red? (cinco semanas)

    Hace _____ _____ que nosotros _____ en la Red.

3.  ¿Cuánto tiempo hace que tú grabas música? (cuatro horas)

    Hace _____ _____ que yo _____ música.

4.  ¿Cuánto tiempo hace que tu hermana visita salones de chat? (diez días)

    Hace _____ _____ que mi hermana _____ salones de chat.

5.  ¿Cuánto tiempo hace que tú y Mariana trabajan en el café?  (seis meses)

    Hace _____ _____ que nosotras _____ en el café.

6.  ¿Cuánto tiempo hace que Jorge y Ana hablan por teléfono? (cuarenta minutos)

    Hace _____ _____ que ellos _____ por teléfono.

**Capítulo 1B**    Fecha _____    **Guided Practice Activities 1B-5**

## Lectura: ¡A bailar! (pp. 62–63)

**A.** The reading in your textbook is about a dance school. Here you will find information about the many dance classes at this school. What kind of information do you expect to find about each class? Some information has already been provided.

1. **Tango:** _____the cost of each class_____ _____

2. **Merengue:** _____ _____

3. **Flamenco:** _____ _____

4. **Swing:** _____ _____

**B.** Read the following schedule from the reading in your textbook. Then, answer the questions that follow.

| Cursos | Día y hora |
|--------|-----------|
| Tango | lunes 17.30h a 18.30h |
| Merengue | martes 17.00h a 18.00h |

1. What course does the school teach on Tuesdays? _____

2. At what time does the tango course begin? _____

**C.** Read the following class descriptions from the schedule in the reading. Then, look at the sentences that follow and write **L** (for **Lectura**) if the sentence tells about something you read. Write **N** (for **No**) if the sentence tells something you didn't read.

*Swing*
*Baila toda la noche con tu pareja este baile muy popular de los Estados Unidos.*

*Tango*
*Ven a aprender este baile romántico de Argentina que se hizo famoso por las composiciones musicales de Gardel y de Piazzolla.*

1. El tango es el baile tradicional de Argentina. _____

2. El swing es un baile popular en los Estados Unidos. _____

3. El tango es un baile romántico de Andalucía. _____

4. El swing se baila con una pareja. _____

**Capítulo 1B**

Fecha _____

# Presentación escrita (p. 65)

**Task:** Your school offers many extracurricular activities. Your teacher wants you to write about the activities you like and why you like them.

❶ **Prewrite.** Look at the following activities and circle the ones that you like to do.

| | | |
|---|---|---|
| jugar al béisbol | usar una computadora | jugar al ajedrez |
| sacar fotos | jugar a los bolos | tocar la guitarra |
| leer libros | hacer gimnasia | cantar en el coro |

❷ **Draft.** Complete the sentences below using some of your answers from **part 1**. Tell why you like those activities, and how long you have been doing them.

1. Me llamo _____ y tengo _____ años.

2. Me gustaría _____ y _____.

3. Me gustan estas actividades porque _____

_____.

4. Hace _____ que _____.

❸ **Revise.** Use the completed sentences from **part 2** to help you write a paragraph. Then, read and check your paragraph by asking the following questions:

- Does my paragraph list two activities?
- Does my paragraph describe the activities?
- Does my paragraph explain why I like these activities?

❹ **Evaluation.** Your teacher may give you a rubric for how the paragraph will be graded. You will probably be graded on:

- how much information you provide about yourself
- use of vocabulary
- accuracy and use of the writing process

# Verbs and expressions that use the infinitive (p. 71)

- Many verbs are often followed by the infinitive. Some of the most common verbs of this type are:

| | | | |
|---|---|---|---|
| **me gusta/gustaría** | *I like/would like* | **querer (e → ie)** | *to want* |
| **me encanta** | *I love* | **pensar (e → ie)** | *to plan to* |
| **poder (o → ue)** | *to be able to* | **necesitar** | *to need* |
| **preferir (e → ie)** | *to prefer* | **tener que** | *to have to* |
| **deber** | *ought to, should* | **ir a** | *to be going to* |

**A.** The sentences below each contain two verbs. Circle the conjugated verb in each sentence and underline the verb in the infinitive. Follow the model.

**Modelo**  Sara (necesita) <u>salir</u> temprano.

1. Rafael y Jorge van a trabajar por la noche.

2. Yo prefiero jugar al fútbol.

3. Tú debes poner la mesa.

4. Oscar piensa hacer una búsqueda en la Red.

5. Nosotros queremos estar de vacaciones.

6. El camarero puede servir ocho bebidas a la vez (*at the same time*).

**B.** Write in the missing word or phrase for each sentence using the cues given in English. Follow the model.

**Modelo** ___*Me*___ ___*encanta*___ bailar la rumba.
            (*I love*)

1. _____ jugar a los bolos.
   (*I prefer*)

2. _____ _____ sacar buenas notas en la escuela.
      (*I have to*)

3. _____ _____ cantar en el coro.
         (*I like*)

4. _____ ir de compras.
      (*I want*)

5. _____ decir la verdad.
   (*I should*)

**Capítulo 2A**

AVSR **2A-2**

# Verbs and expressions that use the infinitive (*continued*)

- The verb **acabar** + **de** + *infinitive* is used to say what someone just finished doing.
  **Alicia acaba de volver.**     *Alicia has just come back.*

**C.** Tell what the people just finished doing by writing forms of **acabar** + **de** + *infinitive* in the blanks. Use the pictures to help you. The first one is done for you.

1.  María _____*acaba*_____ _____*de*_____

    _____*leer*_____ una revista.

2.  Javier _____ _____ _____.

3.  Yo _____ _____ _____
    la guitarra.

4.  Los Rodríguez _____ _____

    _____ en la Red.

**D.** Use the sentence parts to create a complete sentence. Follow the model.

**Modelo**  Yo / tener que / estudiar / esta noche
    *Yo tengo que estudiar esta noche* . _____

1.  Tú / acabar de / almorzar

    _____

2.  Me gustaría / pasar tiempo con mis amigos / mañana

    _____

3.  Alejandro / pensar / visitar a sus primos / durante las vacaciones

    _____

4.  Los buenos estudiantes / deber / practicar el español

    _____

5.  Nosotros / no poder / hacer mucho ruido / en la biblioteca

    _____

**Capítulo 2A**     Fecha _____     **Vocabulary Flash Cards, Sheet 1**

Write the Spanish vocabulary word below each picture. Be sure to include the article for each noun.

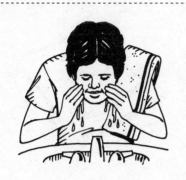

_____

_____

_____

_____

_____

_____

_____

_____

_____

**Capítulo 2A**

Fecha _____ **Vocabulary Flash Cards, Sheet 2**

Write the Spanish vocabulary word or phrase below each picture. Be sure to include the article for each noun.

_____

_____

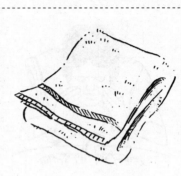

_____

_____

_____

_____

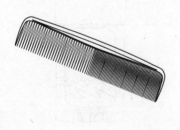

_____

_____

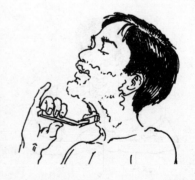

_____

Write the Spanish vocabulary word or phrase below each picture. Be sure to include the article for each noun.

_____

_____

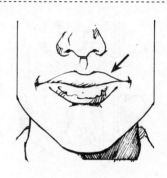

_____

_____

_____

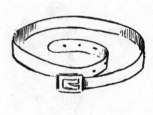

_____

_____

_____

_____

Nombre _____ Hora _____

Fecha _____ **Vocabulary Flash Cards, Sheet 4**

Write the Spanish vocabulary word below each picture. If there is a word or phrase, copy it in the space provided. Be sure to include the article for each noun.

pedir prestado, prestada (a)

el pelo

levantarse

entusiasmado, entusiasmada

nervioso, nerviosa

Copy the word or phrase in the space provided. Be sure to include the article for each noun.

| | | |
|---|---|---|
| **tranquilo, tranquila** <br><br><br><br> _____ , <br> _____ | **las uñas** <br><br><br><br> _____ | **la cita** <br><br><br><br> _____ |
| **ponerse** <br><br><br><br><br> _____ | **prepararse** <br><br><br><br><br> _____ | **antes de** <br><br><br><br> _____ <br> _____ |
| **depende** <br><br><br><br> _____ | **elegante** <br><br><br><br> _____ | **lentamente** <br><br><br><br> _____ |

Copy the word or phrase in the space provided. Be sure to include the article for each noun. These blank cards can be used to write and practice other Spanish vocabulary for the chapter.

| | | |
|---|---|---|
| **luego** <br><br> _____ | **por ejemplo** <br><br> _____ <br><br> _____ | **rápidamente** <br><br> _____ |
| **te ves (bien)** <br><br> _____ _____ <br><br> _____ | **ser** <br><br> _____ | **estar** <br><br> _____ |
| <br><br> _____ | <br><br> _____ | <br><br> _____ |

Tear out this page. Write the English words on the lines. Fold the paper along the dotted line to see the correct answers so you can check your work.

acostarse _____

afeitarse _____

arreglarse (el pelo) _____

bañarse _____

cepillarse
(los dientes) _____

cortarse el pelo _____

despertarse _____

ducharse _____

levantarse _____

lavarse (la cara) _____

pintarse
(las uñas) _____

ponerse _____

prepararse _____

secarse _____

Fold In

Nombre _____   Hora _____

**Capítulo 2A**   Fecha _____   **Vocabulary Check, Sheet 2**

Tear out this page. Write the Spanish words on the lines. Fold the paper along the
dotted line to see the correct answers so you can check your work.

to go to bed          _____

to shave              _____

to fix (one's hair)   _____

to take a bath        _____

to brush
(one's teeth)         _____

to cut one's hair     _____

to wake up            _____

to take a shower      _____

to get up             _____

to wash (one's face)  _____

to paint, to polish
(one's nails)         _____

to put on             _____

to get ready          _____

to dry                _____

Fold In ◄

© Pearson Education, Inc. All rights reserved.

**62** *Guided Practice Activities* ▬ *Vocabulary Check 2A*

**Capítulo 2A**

Fecha _____ **Vocabulary Check, Sheet 3**

Tear out this page. Write the English words on the lines. Fold the paper along the dotted line to see the correct answers so you can check your work.

el agua de colonia _____

el cepillo _____

el cinturón _____

el desodorante _____

la ducha _____

el gel _____

las joyas (de oro, de plata) _____

el maquillaje _____

el peine _____

el pelo _____

el salón de belleza _____

el secador _____

la toalla _____

las uñas _____

Fold In ←

**Capítulo 2A**    Fecha _____    **Vocabulary Check, Sheet 4**

Tear out this page. Write the Spanish words on the lines. Fold the paper along the
dotted line to see the correct answers so you can check your work.

cologne    _____

brush    _____

belt    _____

deodorant    _____

shower    _____

gel    _____

(gold, silver)    _____
jewelry

make-up    _____

comb    _____

hair    _____

beauty salon    _____

blow dryer    _____

towel    _____

nails    _____

Fold In ←

# Reflexive verbs (p. 80)

- You use reflexive verbs to say that people do something to or for themselves. All reflexive verbs in the infinitive form end with **-se**. For example, **secarse el pelo** means "to dry one's hair."
- The reflexive pronouns are **me, te, se, os,** and **nos.** Here is the present-tense form of the reflexive verb **secarse:**

| yo | **me seco** | nosotros/nosotras | **nos secamos** |
|---|---|---|---|
| tú | **te secas** | vosotros/vosotras | **os secáis** |
| usted/él/ella | **se seca** | ustedes/ellos/ellas | **se secan** |

**A.** Look at the underlined word(s) and circle the correct reflexive pronoun for each sentence.

1. <u>Ellos</u> **( nos / se )** lavan el pelo.

2. <u>Tú</u> **( te / se )** pintas las uñas.

3. <u>Javier y yo</u> **( nos / se )** preparamos.

4. <u>Roberto</u> **( nos / se )** viste.

5. <u>Yo</u> **( me / se )** baño.

6. <u>Lola y Rita</u> **( se / nos )** arreglan.

7. <u>Maya</u> **( te / se )** acuesta tarde.

8. <u>Tú</u> **( te / me )** secas el pelo.

**B.** Write the correct reflexive pronoun and form of the verb in parentheses to complete each sentence. Follow the model.

**Modelo** (despertarse) Yo siempre __me__ __despierto__ a las 6:30.

1. (ducharse) Nosotras _____ _____ a las 7:00 de la mañana.

2. (arreglarse) Yo _____ _____ el pelo a las 7:30 de la mañana.

3. (cepillarse) Tú _____ _____ los dientes todos los días.

4. (acostarse) Sandra _____ _____ temprano durante la semana.

5. (secarse)  Uds. _____ _____ después de ducharse.

# Reflexive verbs (*continued*)

- Some verbs can be used in reflexive and non-reflexive forms.

  **Me lavo el pelo todos los días.** *I wash my hair every day.*
  **Lavo el coche.** *I wash the car.*

**C.** Read these sentences. First, circle the whole verb (for example, **lavo** or **me despierto**). Then, write if it is reflexive [**R**] or non-reflexive [**N**]. Follow the model.

**Modelo**   El ruido (despierta) el perro. ___N___

1. Me despierto a las seis. _____        4. Yo me lavo la cara. _____

2. El chico pinta las paredes. _____     5. Yo lavo el carro de mis padres. _____

3. La chica se pinta las uñas. _____

- Reflexive pronouns can be placed before the conjugated verb or attached to the infinitive. These two sentences have the same meaning:

  **Me voy a duchar.** *or* **Voy a ducharme.** *I am going to take a shower.*

**D.** In each sentence, the reflexive pronoun is placed either before the conjugated verb or attached to the infinitive. Rewrite the sentence you are given using the other order without changing the meaning of the sentence. The first one is done for you.

1. Elena se tiene que maquillar. _____*Elena tiene que maquillarse.*_____

2. José se va a duchar. _____

3. Yo voy a arreglarme el pelo. _____

4. Elena e Isabel siempre se tienen que preparar lentamente.

   _____

5. Tú acabas de vestirte. _____

# The verbs *ser* and *estar* (p. 86)

- Remember that the verb **ser** means "to be." Use **ser** to:
  1. describe what a person or thing is or is like (*María **es** simpática.*)
  2. tell where someone or someting is from  (***Soy** de Argentina.*)
  3. tell what something is made of (*El anillo **es** de plata.*)
- Remember that the verb **estar** also means "to be." Use **estar** to:
  1. tell how a person is or feels at the moment (*Elena **está** entusiasmada hoy.*)
  2. tell where a person or thing is located (*Yo **estoy** en el baño.*)

**A.** A student is telling others about the exchange students at school. If the statements tell where the students are from, circle the correct form of **ser**. If the statements tell where the students are, circle the correct form of **estar**.

1. Los estudiantes japoneses ( **son** / **están** ) en la clase.

2. Ellos ( **son** / **están** ) interesantes.

3. Arnaldo ( **es** / **está** ) muy alto y guapo.

4. Arnaldo ( **es** / **está** ) preocupado hoy.

5. Tatiana ( **es** / **está** ) en la cafetería.

**B.** A teacher describes people and things in the school. If the teacher is describing what the things and people are like or what they are made of, then write **son** in the blank. If the teacher describes how the things are or how the people feel, then write **están** in the blank. Follow the model.

**Modelo**   Sara y Jenny _____*están*_____ entusiasmadas hoy.

1. Las joyas _____ de oro.

2. Los anillos _____ elegantes.

3. Ana y Jorge _____ muy nerviosos.

4. Los padres de Mateo _____ inteligentes.

**C.** Complete the conversation using the verbs from the word bank. The first one has been done for you.

| soy | estoy | estás | es | está |
|-----|-------|-------|-----|------|

1. CARMEN: Yo ___soy___ de México. ¿De dónde ___es___ él?

   ELENA: Él _____ de Honduras.

2. CARMEN: Yo _____ nerviosa hoy porque tengo una audición. Y tú, ¿cómo _____ hoy?

   ELENA: Yo _____ muy contenta porque tengo una cita con Rafael.

3. CARMEN: ¿Sí? Yo conozco a Rafael. Él _____ muy simpático. ¿Dónde _____ él?

   ELENA: Rafael _____ en el laboratorio.

# Possessive adjectives (p. 88)

- Spanish possessive adjectives have a long form that comes after the noun:

  **¿Tienes un peine mío?** *Do you have a comb of mine?*
  **El secador es nuestro.** *The dryer is ours.*

- These forms are often used for emphasis:

| mío/mía | míos/mías | nuestro/nuestra | nuestros/nuestras |
|---------|-----------|-----------------|-------------------|
| tuyo/tuya | tuyos/tuyas | vuestro/vuestra | vuestros/vuestras |
| suyo/suya | suyos/suyas | suyo/suya | suyos/suyas |

- Possessive adjectives agree in gender and number with the noun they describe:

  **El peine es mío.** *The comb is mine.*
  **Sara, las tijeras son tuyas, ¿no?** *Sara, the scissors are yours, right?*

**A.** Circle the correct form of the possessive adjectives in parentheses. Follow the model.

Modelo   El jabón es ( (suyo) / suyos ).

1. Los peines son ( mía / **míos** ).

2. Las toallas son ( **nuestras** / nuestro ).

3. El cinturón es ( tuyas / **tuyo** ).

4. Los cepillos son ( mío / **míos** ).

5. El maquillaje es ( **nuestro** / nuestra ).

6. La corbata es ( suyo / **suya** ).

**B.** Read the conversations about who owns various objects. Then, complete each answer with the correct form of the Spanish possessive adjective, using the cues given in English. Follow the model.

Modelo   —¿Es tu secador? *(mine)*
         —Sí, el secador es _____*mío*_____.

1. —¿Es tu toalla? *(mine)*

   —Sí, la toalla es _____.

2. —¿Son estas joyas de tu madre? *(hers)*

   —Sí, las joyas son _____.

3. —¿Son nuestros cepillos? *(ours)*

   —No, los cepillos no son _____.

4. —¿Tienes un cinturón mío? *(yours)*

   —No, no tengo ningún cinturón _____.

Nombre _____ Hora _____

**Capítulo 2A**

Fecha _____

**Guided Practice Activities 2A-5**

## Lectura: El Teatro Colón: Entre bambalinas (pp. 90–91)

**A.** The reading in your textbook is about a theater in Argentina called **El Teatro Colón**. Look at the word below that describes how you feel before giving a performance in such a theater. Then, write four more descriptive words in English.

**nervous,** _____, _____, _____

**B.** How do you think the author of the reading feels about singing and acting in a theater? Look at the following reading selection and underline the words that describe how the author feels.

> *Pasar una noche en el Teatro Colón de Buenos Aires siempre es un evento especial y hoy es muy especial para mí. Vamos a presentar la ópera "La traviata" y voy a cantar en el coro por primera vez. ¡Estoy muy nervioso! ... "La traviata" fue la ópera que se presentó en la inauguración del teatro el 27 de abril de 1857. Por eso estamos muy entusiasmados.*

**C.** Now, read the following advertisement about student auditions from your textbook reading. Then, use the information to decide if the following students are qualified to audition. Circle **Sí** if they are qualified or **No** if they are not qualified.

> ## AUDICIONES
> *para jóvenes de 15 a 25 años de edad.*
> *Si quieres ser músico, cantante o bailarín, tienes talento, eres joven y vives en Buenos Aires, tienes la oportunidad de hacer tus sueños realidad.*

1. José Luis es músico y tiene mucho talento. Él tiene 15 años.
   **(Sí / No)**

2. A Isabel no le gusta bailar ni cantar. Le interesa la tecnología y el arte. Ella tiene 18 años.
   **(Sí / No)**

3. Elena quiere ser bailarina. Ella tiene 13 años.
   **(Sí / No)**

4. Enrique toca la guitarra. Él tiene 30 años y vive en Los Ángeles.
   **(Sí / No)**

5. A Juan le gusta cantar. También sabe tocar el piano. Tiene 25 años.
   **(Sí / No)**

*Guided Practice Activities* — 2A-5 **69**

# Presentación oral (p. 93)

**Task:** Pretend you are an exchange student in Mexico. Your host family wants to know how you celebrate special events in the United States. Bring in a photo from home or from a magazine that shows a special event.

**A.** Look at your photo and use it to answer the following questions.

1. What is the special event? _____

   _____

2. What clothing are people wearing? _____

   _____

3. How do you think the people feel? _____

   _____

**B.** Look again at your photo and your answers from **part A**. Imagine you are going to attend the special event in the photo. How do you get ready? How do you feel before, during, and after the special event? Complete the sentences below in Spanish using your chapter vocabulary.

Me gusta prepararme antes de un evento especial. Primero, yo **1.** _____.

Después, yo **2.** _____. Antes de salir, yo **3.** _____.

Antes de un evento especial yo estoy **4.** _____. En un evento especial,

me gusta estar **5.** _____. Después de un evento, yo estoy

**6.** _____.

**C.** Write your answers in complete sentences from **part B** on index cards. Make sure you describe the event, how you prepare for the event, and how you feel before, during, and after the event.

**D.** Then, practice giving an oral presentation using your completed index cards and your photo. Go through your presentation several times. Try to:

- provide as much information as you can about each point
- use complete sentences
- speak clearly

**Capítulo 2B**

# Cardinal numbers (p. 99)

- Cardinal numbers are used for counting and for telling quantities of things. Remember that **uno** and **cientos** change to agree in gender with the nouns that follow them.

| | |
|---|---|
| **treinta y un perros** | *thirty-one dogs* |
| **seiscientas personas** | *six hundred people* |

**A.** Match the series of numbers on the left with the numerals on the right.

1. _____ mil ochocientos setenta y tres      **a.** 2104

2. _____ cinco mil quinientos      **b.** 1707

3. _____ mil setecientos siete      **c.** 1873

4. _____ mil cuatrocientos noventa y dos      **d.** 5500

5. _____ dos mil ciento cuatro      **e.** 1928

6. _____ mil novecientos veintiocho      **f.** 1492

**B.** Write the numbers indicated numerically. Follow the model.

**Modelo** ciento cuarenta y seis     *146*

1. trescientos treinta y tres     _____

2. mil ochenta y cinco     _____

3. dos mil novecientos     _____

4. quinientos setenta y seis     _____

5. ciento cuarenta y cuatro mil     _____

6. doscientos noventa y ocho     _____

7. cincuenta mil veinticinco     _____

8. nueve mil seiscientos treinta     _____

Write the Spanish vocabulary word below each picture. Be sure to include the article for each noun.

_____

_____

_____

_____

_____

_____

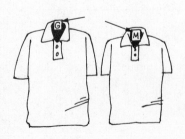

_____

_____

_____

Write the Spanish vocabulary word below each picture. If there is a word or phrase, copy it in the space provided. Be sure to include the article for each noun.

**flojo, floja**   **apretado, apretada**   **vivo, viva**

_____ ,   _____ ,   _____ ,
_____   _____   _____

Copy the word or phrase in the space provided. Be sure to include the article for each noun.

| | | |
|---|---|---|
| **la liquidación** <br><br> _____ | **tan + *adjective*** <br><br> _____ <br><br> _____ | **me/te importa(n)** <br><br> _____ |
| **claro, clara** <br><br> _____, <br> _____ | **de sólo un color** <br><br> _____ _____ <br> _____ | **oscuro, oscura** <br><br> _____, <br> _____ |
| **pastel** <br><br> _____ | **¿De qué está hecho, hecha?** <br><br> _____ _____ <br> _____ _____, | **Está hecho, hecha de...** <br><br> _____ _____ <br> _____ _____, |

Copy the word or phrase in the space provided. Be sure to include the article for each noun.

| | | |
|---|---|---|
| **algodón** | **cuero** | **lana** |
| _____ | _____ | _____ |
| **seda** | **tela sintética** | **alto, alta** |
| | _____ | _____, |
| _____ | _____ | _____ |
| **bajo, baja** | **gastar** | **el precio** |
| _____, | | |
| _____ | _____ | _____ |

Copy the word or phrase in the space provided. Be sure to include the article for each noun.

| | | |
|---|---|---|
| **escoger** | **estar de moda** | **el estilo** |
| _____ | _____ _____ | _____ |
| **exagerado, exagerada** | **mediano, mediana** | **probarse** |
| _____, _____ | _____, _____ | _____ |
| **anunciar** | **encontrar** | **en realidad** |
| _____ | _____ | _____ _____ |

**Capítulo 2B**    Fecha _____    **Vocabulary Flash Cards, Sheet 6**

Copy the word or phrase in the space provided. Be sure to include the article for each noun. These blank cards can be used to write and practice other Spanish vocabulary for the chapter.

| | | |
|---|---|---|
| **inmediatamente**<br><br><br><br>_____ | **me parece que**<br><br><br>_____ _____ | **¿Qué te parece?**<br><br><br>_____ _____<br><br>_____ |
| **recientemente**<br><br><br><br>_____ | **el cheque de viajero**<br><br><br>_____ _____<br>_____ _____ | <br><br><br>_____ |
| <br><br><br><br>_____ | <br><br><br>_____ | <br><br><br>_____ |

These blank cards can be used to write and practice other Spanish vocabulary for the chapter.

_____   _____   _____

_____   _____   _____

_____   _____   _____

Tear out this page. Write the English words on the lines. Fold the paper along the dotted line to see the correct answers so you can check your work.

la entrada _____

la ganga _____

el letrero _____

la liquidación _____

el mercado _____

la salida _____

el cajero, la cajera _____

el cheque (personal) _____

el cheque de viajero _____

el cupón de regalo _____

en efectivo _____

el precio _____

la marca _____

la talla _____

Fold In →

**Capítulo 2B**   Fecha _____   **Vocabulary Check, Sheet 2**

Tear out this page. Write the Spanish words on the lines. Fold the paper along the dotted line to see the correct answers so you can check your work.

entrance _____

bargain _____

sign _____

sale _____

market _____

exit _____

cashier _____

(personal) check _____

traveler's check _____

gift certificate _____

cash _____

price _____

brand _____

size _____

Fold In ←

Tear out this page. Write the English words on the lines. Fold the paper along the dotted line to see the correct answers so you can check your work.

algodón  _____

cuero  _____

lana  _____

seda  _____

tela sintética  _____

apretado, apretada  _____

flojo, floja  _____

mediano, mediana  _____

estar de moda  _____

encontrar  _____

anunciar  _____

escoger  _____

probarse  _____

comprar  _____

Fold In →

Tear out this page. Write the Spanish words on the lines. Fold the paper along the dotted line to see the correct answers so you can check your work.

cotton                  _____

leather                 _____

wool                    _____

silk                    _____

synthetic fabric        _____

tight                   _____

loose                   _____

medium                  _____

to be in fashion        _____

to find                 _____

to announce             _____

to choose               _____

to try on               _____

to buy                  _____

Fold In ←

# Preterite of regular verbs (p. 110)

- Use the preterite tense to talk about actions that were completed in the past. To form the preterite tense of a regular verb, add the preterite endings to the stem of the verb.
- Here are the preterite forms for the verbs **mirar** (*to look*), **aprender** (*to learn*), and **escribir** (*to write*):

| | | | | | |
|---|---|---|---|---|---|
| yo | **miré**<br>**aprendí**<br>**escribí** | *I looked*<br>*I learned*<br>*I wrote* | nosotros/<br>nosotras | **miramos**<br>**aprendimos**<br>**escribimos** | *we looked*<br>*we learned*<br>*we wrote* |
| tú | **miraste**<br>**aprendiste**<br>**escribiste** | *you looked*<br>*you learned*<br>*you wrote* | vosotros/<br>vosotras | **mirasteis**<br>**aprendisteis**<br>**escribisteis** | *you looked*<br>*you learned*<br>*you wrote* |
| usted/<br>él/ella | **miró**<br>**aprendió**<br>**escribió** | *you/he/she looked*<br>*you/he/she learned*<br>*you/he/she wrote* | ustedes/<br>ellos/ellas | **miraron**<br>**aprendieron**<br>**escribieron** | *you/they looked*<br>*you/they learned*<br>*you/they wrote* |

**A.** Read the sentences below. If they tell what happens regularly in the present (using the present tense), write a **1**. If they tell what happened in the past (using the preterite tense), write a **2**. Follow the model.

**Modelo**   Yo aprendí a leer.   _____2_____

1. Tú miraste el letrero.   _____
2. Mi papá escribió un cheque.   _____
3. Las chicas estudian mucho en la clase.   _____
4. Uds. escriben el libro.   _____
5. Yo miré la tele anoche.   _____

**B.** Write the appropriate ending to complete each verb stem. Follow the model.

**Modelo**   (comer) Nosotros com _imos_ en la cafetería.

1. (aprender)   Uds. aprend_____ a leer en la escuela.
2. (escribir)   Yo no escrib_____ la carta.
3. (aprender)   Carlos y yo aprend_____ el inglés.
4. (mirar)   Rafael no mir_____ el precio de la camisa.
5. (enviar)   Mis abuelos me envi_____ una carta.
6. (comer)   Tú com_____ con Antonio anoche, ¿verdad?
7. (preparar)   Mi padre prepar_____ la comida.

# Preterite of regular verbs (*continued*)

- Note that -**ar** and -**er** verbs that have a stem change in the present tense do not have a stem change in the preterite.

    Present tense: **Siempre encuentro gangas en el mercado.**
    *I always find bargains at the market.*

    Preterite tense: **Ayer no encontraste gangas en el mercado.**
    *Yesterday you didn't find bargains at the market.*

**C.** Complete the following paragraph by filling in each blank with the correct preterite form of the verb in parentheses. The first one is done for you.

La semana pasada yo _____*fui*_____ (**ir**) al centro comercial, pero yo no _____

(**encontrar**) una camiseta de mi talla porque soy grande. Mi mamá también buscó la

camiseta ayer pero _____ (**costar**) mucho dinero. Recientemente, me _____

(**probar**) una camiseta apretada y no me gustó. Esta mañana nosotros _____

_____ (**despertarse**) temprano para ir de compras. ¡Qué bien, porque yo

_____ (**volver**) a la tienda y compré mi camiseta!

- Verbs that end in -**car**, -**gar**, and -**zar** have a spelling change in the **yo** form of the preterite.
- Other preterite forms of these verbs are regular.

| buscar | c → qu | yo busqué | él/ella | buscó | ellos/ellas | buscaron |
| pagar | g → gu | yo pagué | él/ella | pagó | ellos/ellas | pagaron |
| almorzar | z → c | yo almorcé | él/ella | almorzó | ellos/ellas | almorzaron |

**D.** Read the following conversation. Circle the verb in each question. Then, write the appropriate form of that same verb in the blank. The first one has been done for you.

1. JUAN: ¿(Buscaste) una camisa nueva?

    EMILIO: Sí, yo ____*busqué*____ una camisa nueva. Tere _____ zapatos.

2. JUAN: ¿Pagaste la camisa en efectivo?

    EMILIO: Sí, yo _____ en efectivo. Miguel _____ con tarjeta de crédito.

3. JUAN: ¿Almorzaste con Elena en el restaurante?

    EMILIO: Sí, yo _____ con Elena. Nosotros _____ a las dos.

4. Juan: ¿Llegaste temprano a la tienda?

    Emilio: Sí, yo _____ a las nueve. Emilia y Víctor _____ tarde.

# Demonstrative adjectives (p. 114)

- Demonstrative adjectives show how close something is to the speaker. Here's a chart that compares the demonstrative adjectives:

| Singular | | Plural | |
|---|---|---|---|
| **este/esta** | *this* | **estos/estas** | *these* |
| **ese/esa** | *that* | **esos/esas** | *those* |
| **aquel/aquella** | *that (over there)* | **aquellos/aquellas** | *those (over there)* |

**A.** Write the equivalent word(s) in English for each underlined demonstrative adjective. Follow the model.

**Modelo**    Me gustan <u>aquellas</u> camisas blancas.  *English:* <u>those (over there)</u>

1. Yo prefiero <u>estas</u> camisas rojas. *English:* _____

2. A mí me gusta <u>esta</u> gorra roja. *English:* _____

3. Yo quiero comprar <u>esos</u> zapatos. *English:* _____

4. A mi madre le gusta <u>aquella</u> blusa elegante. *English:* _____

5. Ella compró <u>ese</u> bolso cuando fue a París. *English:* _____

**B.** Circle the correct demonstrative adjective in parentheses to complete the dialogue. Remember adjectives must agree in gender and number with the noun they describe.

LUPE:  Mamá, ¡mira **( este / esta )** suéter de lana! Es perfecto para papá.

MADRE:  Sí, pero él prefiere **( esos / esas )** pantalones azules allí. Son más prácticos.

LUPE:  ¡Oh! Quiero comprar **( aquellos / aquellas )** faldas bonitas cerca de la ventana.

MADRE:  Me gustan, pero **( este / esta )** falda es tu número, el dos.

LUPE:  Pero no va bien con **( ese / esa )** camisa que me gusta, la roja.

MADRE:  Entonces, prueba las dos.

LUPE:  Bien. Gracias, mamá.

Nombre _____     Hora _____

**Capítulo 2B**     Fecha _____     **Guided Practice Activities 2B-3a**

# Demonstrative adjectives (*continued*)

**C.** Look at the pictures of clothing below. Then, answer the question by writing in the correct demonstrative adjective for each article of clothing. The smallest article of clothing is the farthest away. Follow the model.

**Modelo**
—¿Qué falda prefieres?
—Prefiero ___*aquella*___ falda.

1.
—¿Qué camisa vas a comprar?
—Voy a comprar _____ camisa.

2.
—¿Qué pantalones te gustan?
—Me gustan _____ pantalones.

3.
—¿Qué traje prefieres?
—Prefiero _____ traje.

4.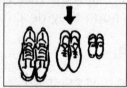
—¿Qué zapatos piensas comprar?
—Pienso comprar _____ zapatos.

**D.** Write the correct demonstrative adjectives based on the English cues you are given.

1. (*this*)            Debes leer _____ libro. Es muy interesante.

2. (*those over there*)   ¿Quiénes son _____ señoritas?

3. (*that*)            ¿Leíste _____ novela antes?

4. (*these*)          ¿De quiénes son _____ cheques de viajero?

5. (*this*)            No me gusta _____ lápiz. Prefiero uno azul.

# Using adjectives as nouns (p. 116)

- When you compare two similar things, you can avoid repetition by dropping the noun and using the *article* + the *adjective* for the second thing.

  **¿Cuál prefieres, el vestido apretado o el flojo?** *Which do you prefer, the tight dress or the loose one?*

  **Prefiero el flojo.** *I prefer the loose one.*

**A.** Read the questions below. Circle the noun in each question. Then, answer the questions using the appropriate article and adjective as a noun.

**Modelo** —¿Pagaste el (precio) alto o el bajo?

—Pagué __*el*__ __*bajo*__ .

1. —¿Compraste la blusa clara o la oscura?

   —Compré _____ _____ .

2. —¿Probaste los zapatos caros o los baratos?

   —Probé _____ _____ .

3. —¿Encontraste el vestido grande o el mediano?

   —Encontré _____ _____ .

4. —¿Te gustan los jeans apretados o los flojos?

   —Me gustan _____ _____ .

**B.** Read the sentences below. Complete the second sentence in each pair using an article and the opposite adjective as a noun. Choose from the word bank. Follow the model.

| antipáticos | ~~blanca~~ | claro | floja | largas | pequeñas |
|---|---|---|---|---|---|

**Modelo** A Juan le encanta la ropa negra. No le encanta __*la*__ __*blanca*__

1. Nosotros preferimos las tiendas grandes. No preferimos _____ _____ .

2. A ellas les gustan los cajeros simpáticos. No les gustan _____ _____ .

3. Yo no me pruebo la ropa apretada. Me pruebo _____ _____ .

4. Emily no prefiere las faldas cortas. Prefiere _____ _____ .

5. No compraste el traje oscuro. Compraste _____ _____ .

# Lectura: Los jeans (pp. 118–119)

**A.** The reading in your textbook is about the history of jeans. Before you read the selection, think about and answer the following questions.

**1.** Do you like to wear jeans? Why? _____

**2.** Why are jeans popular with many students? _____

**B.** The second section from your textbook reading is about one of the inventors of jeans. Read the selection and answer the questions. Use the *Hints* below to help you answer the questions.

> ### Un poco de historia
> *Levi Strauss, un joven alemán, llegó a los Estados Unidos con su familia en 1847 a la edad de 18 años. Después de trabajar algunos años con su familia, Strauss viajó a California para abrir una tienda de ropa y accesorios. Esta tienda se convirtió en un negocio próspero durante los siguientes 20 años, y Strauss se hizo rico.*

**1.** What type of store did Levi Strauss open in California? *Hint:* Look for the words **una tienda de.**

_____

**2.** What happened over the next 20 years? *Hint:* Look for the words **próspero** and **rico.**

_____

**C.** Now, look at the dates and events from the life of Levi Strauss and answer the following questions.

**1847:** Levi Strauss llegó a los Estados Unidos.
**1872:** Recibió una carta de Jacob Davis que le explicó un proceso para hacer más fuertes los pantalones. Ellos pidieron la patente de este proceso.
**1873:** Recibieron la patente y empezaron a fabricar *waist overalls.*

**1.** When did Levi Strauss arrive in the United States?

    **a.** 1873                **b.** 1847

**2.** Before Levi Strauss and Jacob Davis began to make waist overalls, they needed a

    **a.** patent.             **b.** letter.

**3.** When Strauss and Davis received the patent, they began to

    **a.** make waist overalls.     **b.** explain the process.

# Presentación escrita (p. 121)

**Task:** You received $200 for your birthday and have just purchased some articles of clothing. Write an e-mail to your friend describing your shopping trip.

**A.** Before you write the e-mail, it would be helpful to organize the information about your purchases. Fill in the table below. The first line is done for you.

| | ¿Qué compraste? | ¿Dónde...? | ¿Cuánto pagaste? |
|---|---|---|---|
| 1. | camiseta | en el centro comercial | $20 |
| 2. | _____ | _____ | _____ |
| 3. | _____ | _____ | _____ |

**B.** Answer the following questions about your shopping trip. You can look back at your answers in **part A** to help you.

1. ¿Qué compraste?

   Yo _____.

2. ¿Dónde compraste la ropa?

   Yo _____.

3. ¿Cuánto pagaste?

   Yo _____.

4. ¿Por qué compraste esta ropa?

   Yo _____.

**C.** Use the answers to the questions in **parts A** and **B** to write an e-mail to your friend below. You may use the following model.

iHola _____! Yo recibí _____ en mi cumpleaños. Yo compré ropa
en el _____. Compré _____ Yo pagué _____
Luego, compré _____. Pagué _____ por _____
_____ está de moda y me gusta mucho. ¿Qué te parece mi
ropa? Adiós, _____

**D.** Check your e-mail for spelling, forms of the preterite, and agreement. Then, send it to your teacher or a classmate.

# Telling time

- Remember that to tell time, you use **es** or **son** + numbers and time expressions. Some common time-telling expressions are:

| y | Son las cinco **y** veinte. | *It's twenty after five (5:20).* |
|---|---|---|
| **cuarto** | Son las dos y **cuarto**. | *It's quarter after two (2:15).* |
| **media** | Es la una y **media**. | *It's one thirty (1:30).* |
| **menos** | Son las doce **menos** cuarto. | *It's quarter of twelve (11:45).* |

**A.** Fill in the blanks with the words necessary to complete the times shown in the drawings. The first one is done for you.

1. `3:05` Son _____ *las* _____ tres _____ *y* _____ cinco.

2. `5:15` Son las cinco _____ _____.

3. `4:10` Son _____ cuatro _____ diez.

4. `8:52` Son las _____ _____ ocho.

5. `6:30` Son _____ seis y _____.

- Use *a* in order to tell at what time you do something or something takes place. Use *de* to tell what part of the day it is.

| **¿A qué hora es la clase de español?** | *At what time is Spanish class?* |
|---|---|
| *A* las nueve y media *de* la mañana. | *At nine thirty in the morning (AM).* |
| *A* la una *de* la tarde. | *At one o'clock in the afternoon (PM).* |

**B.** Look at the television listings below and answer the questions that follow.

| 6:30 AM | Las noticias | 12:00 PM | Plaza Sésamo | 6:55 PM | Concierto |
|---|---|---|---|---|---|
| 7:15 AM | El tiempo | 1:30 PM | Telenovelas | | |

**Modelo** ¿A qué hora es Plaza Sésamo? _____ *A las doce de la tarde* _____.

1. ¿A qué hora es el concierto? _____.

2. ¿A qué hora son las noticias? _____.

3. ¿A qué hora son las telenovelas? _____.

4. ¿A qué hora es el tiempo? _____.

Write the Spanish vocabulary word or phrase below each picture. Be sure to include the article for each noun.

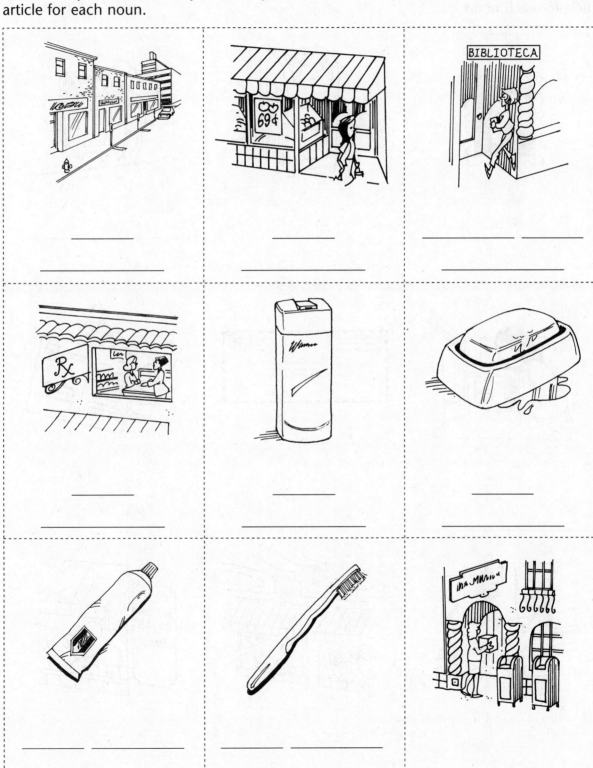

Write the Spanish vocabulary word or phrase below each picture. Be sure to include the article for each noun.

**Capítulo 3A**     Fecha _____     **Vocabulary Flash Cards, Sheet 3**

Write the Spanish vocabulary word or phrase below each picture. Be sure to include the article for each noun.

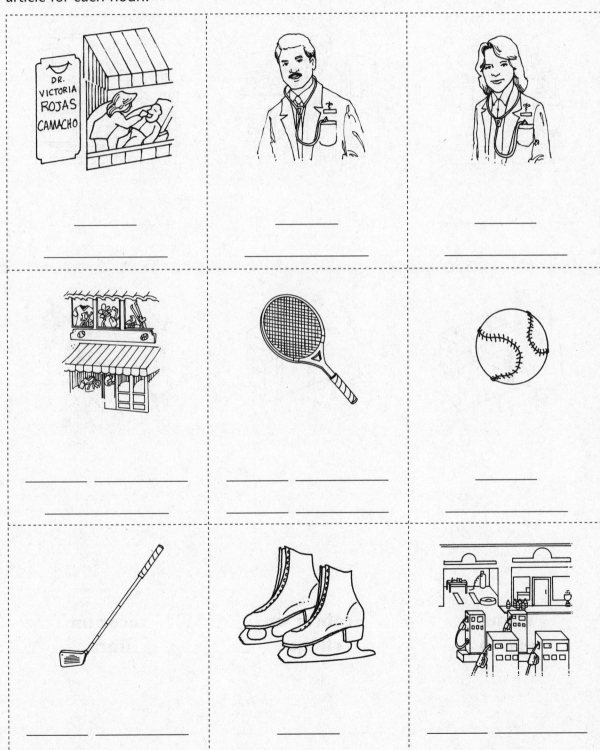

Write the Spanish vocabulary word below each picture. If there is a word or phrase, copy it in the space provided. Be sure to include the article for each noun.

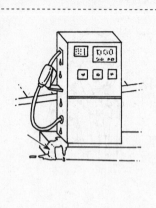

_____
_____

_____

_____

_____
_____

_____

_____

**se me olvidó**

_____
_____

**cobrar un cheque**

_____
_____

**sacar un libro**

_____
_____

Copy the word or phrase in the space provided. Be sure to include the article for each noun.

| **caramba** | **casi** | **¡Cómo no!** |
|:---:|:---:|:---:|
| _____ | _____ | _____ |
| **en seguida** | **hasta** | **por** |
| _____ | _____ | _____ |
| **pronto** | **Hasta pronto.** | **quedarse** |
| _____ | _____ | _____ |

Copy the word or phrase in the space provided. Be sure to include the article for each noun. These blank cards can be used to write and practice other Spanish vocabulary for the chapter.

| | | |
|---|---|---|
| **todavía**<br><br>_____ | **varios,<br>varias**<br><br>_____ ,<br>_____ | **cerrar**<br><br>_____ |
| **la<br>gasolina**<br><br>_____ | _____ | _____ |
| _____ | _____ | _____ |

Tear out this page. Write the English words on the lines. Fold the paper along the dotted line to see the correct answers so you can check your work.

la farmacia                _____

el supermercado       _____

el banco                   _____

el centro                   _____

la estación
de servicio               _____

enviar                      _____

el sello                    _____

la tarjeta                  _____

el buzón                  _____

todavía                   _____

cerrar                     _____

cuidar a                  _____

devolver (un libro)    _____

Hasta pronto.          _____

ir a pie                   _____

Fold In

Tear out this page. Write the Spanish words on the lines. Fold the paper along the dotted line to see the correct answers so you can check your work.

pharmacy _____

supermarket _____

bank _____

downtown _____

service station _____

to send _____

stamp _____

card _____

mailbox _____

still _____

to close _____

to take care of _____

to return (a book) _____

See you soon. _____

to go on foot _____

Fold In

Tear out this page. Write the English words on the lines. Fold the paper along the dotted line to see the correct answers so you can check your work.

la carta _____

echar una carta _____

el correo _____

el equipo deportivo _____

el palo de golf _____

los patines _____

la pelota _____

la raqueta de tenis _____

el cepillo de dientes _____

el champú _____

el jabón _____

la pasta dental _____

caramba _____

casi _____

Fold In

Tear out this page. Write the Spanish words on the lines. Fold the paper along the dotted line to see the correct answers so you can check your work.

letter                    _____

to mail a letter          _____

post office               _____

sports equipment          _____

golf club                 _____

skates                    _____

ball                      _____

tennis racket             _____

toothbrush                _____

shampoo                   _____

soap                      _____

toothpaste                _____

good gracious             _____

almost                    _____

Fold In →

**Capítulo 3A**

# Direct object pronouns (p. 138)

- A direct object tells who or what receives the action of the verb. Direct objects may represent people or things.
- To avoid repeating a direct object noun, you can replace it with a direct object pronoun.

    **¿Martín echó la carta ayer?** (**Carta** is the direct object noun.)

    **No, la echó hoy.** (**La** is the direct object pronoun. It replaces the word **carta**.)

- Here are the direct object pronouns you have already used:

| Singular | Plural |
|---|---|
| **lo** it, him, you *(masculine formal)* | **los** them, you *(masculine formal)* |
| **la** it, her, you *(feminine formal)* | **las** them, you *(feminine formal)* |

**A.** Circle the direct object noun in each sentence. Then, write the direct object pronoun that replaces the circled words. Follow the model.

**Modelo** Margarita cobró el (cheque) _____ lo _____

1. Paquito pasó la aspiradora ayer. _____

2. Juanucho buscó los patines. _____

3. Tú llenaste el tanque del coche. _____

4. Yo envié las tarjetas a la tía. _____

5. Uds. sacaron los libros de la biblioteca. _____

6. Ella cerró la estación de servicio. _____

**B.** Look at the sentences from exercise A. Replace the direct object noun you circled with the pronoun that corresponds to it. Follow the model.

**Modelo** Margarita _____ lo _____ cobró.

1. Paquito _____ pasó ayer.

2. Juanucho _____ buscó.

3. Tú _____ llenaste.

4. Yo _____ envié a la tía.

5. Uds. _____ sacaron de la biblioteca.

6. Ella _____ cerró.

# Direct object pronouns (*continued*)

**C.** Circle the direct object noun in each question. Then, answer each question by using a direct object pronoun in your answer. Use the verbs given. Follow the model.

**Modelo**    ¿Él cobró el (cheque) el martes pasado?

Sí, ___lo___ ___cobró___ el martes pasado.

1. ¿Ella pasó la aspiradora ayer? Sí, _____ _____ ayer.

2. ¿Ellos arreglaron el cuarto esta semana? No, no _____ _____ esta semana.

3. ¿Quién echó la carta en el buzón? Anita _____ _____ en el buzón.

4. ¿Quién envió las tarjetas de cumpleaños? Billy _____ _____ .

5. ¿Ellas sacaron los libros de la biblioteca? Sí, _____ _____ de la bilbioteca.

6. ¿Jenny y Miguel cerraron la estación de servicio? No, no _____ _____ .

7. ¿Él lavó los platos anoche? Sí, _____ _____ anoche.

> • The direct object pronoun is placed before conjugated verbs. When an infinitive is present, the pronoun may come before the conjugated verb *or* attached to the infinitive.
>
> **Lo tengo que hacer.**   *or*   **Tengo que hacerlo.**

**D.** Rewrite the following sentences to show a second possibility for where the direct object pronouns can be placed. Follow the model.

**Modelo**    ¿La raqueta? La voy a comprar mañana.    ___Voy a comprarla mañana___ .

1. ¿Las cartas? Las vamos a echar hoy.    _____ .

2. ¿El palo de golf? Lo tengo que comprar.    _____ .

3. ¿Los patines? Los vas a usar esta tarde.    _____ .

4. ¿La mesa? La voy a poner hoy.    _____ .

5. ¿Los periódicos? Los voy a separar esta noche.    _____ .

6. ¿El dentista? Lo tengo que visitar hoy.    _____ .

# Irregular preterite verbs: *ir, ser* (p. 140)

- The preterite forms of **ser** (*to be*) and **ir** (*to go*) are the same.

| yo | **fui** | nosotros/nosotras | **fuimos** |
|---|---|---|---|
| tú | **fuiste** | vosotros/vosotras | **fuisteis** |
| usted/él/ella | **fue** | ustedes/ellos/ellas | **fueron** |

- Usually the context of the verb is what makes the meaning clear:
   **Mi doctora fue la Dra. Serrano.** *My doctor was Dr. Serrano.*
   **El año pasado fue muy difícil.** *Last year was very difficult.*
   **Yo fui a la farmacia.** *I went to the pharmacy.*
   (If you see the preposition "**a**" following one of these verb forms, the verb is **ir** and the meaning is "*went*".)

**A.** Circle the correct conjugated verb in parentheses.

> ¡Hola Margarita!
>
> Ayer ( **fuimos** / **fue** ) un día muy interesante. Primero, mi
> familia y yo ( **fuimos** / **fue** ) al parque zoológico. Mis padres
> ( **fueron** / **fue** ) a ver los monos y mis hermanos y yo
> ( **fueron** / **fuimos** ) a comer un helado. ¡( **Fuimos** / **Fue** )
> delicioso! A las cinco todos nosotros ( **fueron** / **fuimos** )
> a comer en un restaurante argentino. La comida ( **fui** / **fue** )
> fantástica y yo ( **fuiste** / **fui** ) a la casa muy contenta.
> ¿Y tú? ¿Adónde ( **fue** / **fuiste** ) ayer?
> Un abrazo
> —Victoria

## Irregular preterite verbs: *ir, ser* (*continued*)

**B.** Write the correct form of the verb within parentheses. Follow the model.

**Modelo**   Rafael y Hernando no _____*fueron*_____ (**ir**) al consultorio ayer.

1. Anoche yo _____ (**ir**) al centro.

2. Luego, Marcela y yo _____ (**ir**) a cobrar un cheque.

3. La noche _____ (**ser**) divertida.

4. Y tú ¿adónde _____ (**ir**)?

5. La tarde _____ (**ser**) aburrida.

6. Ellos _____ (**ir**) a un concierto en el parque.

7. El plato principal _____ (**ser**) bistec y papas.

8. Nosotras _____ (**ir**) a la playa.

## Irregular preterite verbs: *hacer, tener, estar, poder* (p. 142)

- The preterite of the irregular verbs **hacer** (*to do*) and **tener** (*to have*) follow a similar pattern.

| yo | hice<br>tuve | nosotros/nosotras | hicimos<br>tuvimos |
|---|---|---|---|
| tú | hiciste<br>tuviste | vosotros/vosotras | hicisteis<br>tuvisteis |
| usted/él/ella | hizo<br>tuvo | ustedes/ellos/ellas | hicieron<br>tuvieron |

**A.** Complete the dialogue by circling the correct form of the verb within parentheses. The first one is done for you.

1. LAURA: ¿Qué (**hicieron**/ **hizo** ) tú y tu familia ayer?

   DANIEL: Nosotros ( **tuvimos** / **tuvieron** ) que ir al centro.

2. LAURA: ¿Qué ( **hizo** / **hice** ) tu papá?

   DANIEL: Él ( **tuve** / **tuvo** ) que enviar una carta.

3. LAURA: ¿Qué ( **hiciste** / **hizo** ) tu mamá?

   DANIEL: Ella ( **tuvo** / **tuve** ) que devolver un libro.

4. DANIEL: Y tú Laura, ¿qué ( **hizo** / **hiciste** ) en la noche?

   LAURA: Yo ( **tuve** / **tuviste** ) que cuidar a mi hermanito.

## Irregular preterite verbs: *hacer, tener, estar, poder* (*continued*)

- Like the verbs **hacer** and **tener**, the verbs **estar** (*to be*) and **poder** (*to be able*) are also irregular in the preterite.
- Unlike regular preterite verbs, **hacer, tener, estar,** and **poder** do not have accent marks on their preterite forms.
- Here are the preterite forms of **estar** and **poder**:

| yo | estuve | nosotros/nosotras | estuvimos |
|---|---|---|---|
| tú | estuviste | vosotros/vosotras | estuvisteis |
| usted/él/ella | estuvo | ustedes/ellos/ellas | estuvieron |

| yo | pude | nosotros/nosotras | pudimos |
|---|---|---|---|
| tú | pudiste | vosotros/vosotras | pudisteis |
| usted/él/ella | pudo | ustedes/ellos/ellas | pudieron |

**B.** Write the missing endings of the preterite forms of **estar** and **poder** in the sentences below.

1. Ayer yo estuv_____ en el parque por una hora.
2. Mi amigo Pablo no pud_____ venir.
3. Pablo y su papá estuv_____ en la oficina del doctor.
4. Después, Pablo no pud_____ ir a la escuela.
5. Él estuv_____ enfermo por tres días.
6. Tú estuv_____ enfermo también, ¿no?

**C.** Complete the sentences below with the correct preterite form of the verb in parentheses. Follow the model.

**Modelo**   Yo ___hice___ (**hacer**) mucha tarea anoche.

1. El fin de semana pasado, yo _____ (**estar**) en casa.
2. Mi hermano Tito _____ (**tener**) que hacer una tarjeta para nuestro tío, Julio.
3. Tito casi no _____ (**poder**) terminarla a tiempo.
4. Después, echó la tarjeta al buzón y por la noche, nosotros _____ (**hacer**) la cena.
5. ¿Dónde _____ (**estar**) Uds. el fin de semana?

**Capítulo 3A**    Fecha _____

# Lectura: La unidad en la comunidad internacional (pp. 146–147)

**A.** The reading in your textbook is about **Ciudades Hermanas Internacional** or the Sister Cities program. As you look at the reading, you will notice several headings. Headings are a way of organizing ideas in a reading. Look at the headings below from the reading to help you complete the following activity.

> *Ciudades Hermanas Internacional*
> *¡Quiero tener una ciudad hermana!*
> *Intercambio económico*
> *Intercambio cultural*
> *Intercambio educativo*

Now, write **L** (for **Lectura**) next to the sentence below if it is something you might find in the reading. Write **N** (for **No**) next to the sentence if it is something you might not find in the reading.

1. The Sister Cities International program is for sports teams. _____

2. The mission of the Sister Cities International program is exchange and cooperation. _____

3. The sister cities can have educational, economic, and cultural exchanges. _____

4. How to have a sister city. _____

5. Sister cities cannot be from different countries. _____

**B.** Read the following excerpt from the reading in your textbook. Then, determine the important ideas of the excerpt and place a ✓ next to them.

> *¡Quiero tener una ciudad hermana!*
> *Cualquier (Any) ciudad en los Estados Unidos puede tener una ciudad hermana. Primero es necesario encontrar otra ciudad extranjera (foreign). Esta ciudad puede tener alguna relación con la ciudad original. Por ejemplo, ciudades que tienen el mismo nombre, como Toledo, Ohio y Toledo, España, pueden asociarse. También, las ciudades que celebran el mismo festival pueden formar relaciones de hermandad.*

1. It is difficult for people in the United States to find a sister city. _____

2. People in the United States can easily find a sister city. _____

3. Cities with the same names can become sister cities. _____

4. Cities that don't celebrate the same festivals can become sister cities. _____

# Presentación oral (p. 149)

**Task:** Pretend you need to prepare for a trip to Mérida, Mexico. You will visit some Mayan ruins and the beach in Cancún. Remember that it will be very hot and humid.

**A.** Complete the following chart. In the **¿Lo necesitas?** column, write **Sí** if you need the item or **No** if you do not need the item. Then, place a ✓ in the right column, **¿Lo tienes?**, if you already have the item.

| Ropa | ¿Lo necesitas? | ¿Lo tienes? |
|---|---|---|
| pantalones cortos | | |
| camisetas | | |
| abrigo | | |
| traje de baño | | |
| sombrero para el sol | | |
| botas | | |
| cepillo de dientes | | |

**B.** Review your answers in **part A**. List three items that you need but that you already have at home.

1. _____   2. _____   3. _____

**C.** Pretend you already went shopping for the items you did not have. In the left column, list those items you had to buy for your trip. In the right column, write down where you bought them. The first one is done for you.

| Tuve que comprar... | ¿Dónde? |
|---|---|
| *pantalones cortos* | *el almacén* |
| | |
| | |
| | |

**D.** Use the information in **parts B** and **C** to talk about your trip preparation. Tell what you need and what you have or don't have. You may also bring in and show articles of clothing as props. You can use the following as a model.

*Para mi viaje a México necesito camisetas, pero ya las tengo.*
*Tuve que comprar unos pantalones cortos en el almacén...*

# The verbs *salir*, *decir*, and *venir* (p. 155)

- Salir, decir, and **venir** are three -ir verbs that have irregular **yo** forms in the present tense (**salgo, digo,** and **vengo**). **Decir** and **venir** follow stem-changing patterns **e → i** and **e → ie**.

| yo | salgo | *I left* | nosotros/<br>nosotras | salimos | *we left* |
|---|---|---|---|---|---|
| | digo | *I said, I told* | | decimos | *we said, we told* |
| | vengo | *I came* | | venimos | *we came* |
| tú | sales | *you left* | vosotros/<br>vosotras | salís | *you left* |
| | dices | *you said, you told* | | decís | *you said, you told* |
| | vienes | *you came* | | venís | *you came* |
| usted/<br>él/ella | sale | *you/he/she left* | ustedes/<br>ellos/ellas | salen | *you/they left* |
| | dice | *you/he/she said; told* | | dicen | *you/they said; told* |
| | viene | *you/he/she came* | | vienen | *you/they came* |

**A.** Circle the correct form of the verb in parentheses. Follow the model.

**Modelo**    Yo ( salgo / sale ) de la casa.

1. Nosotros ( **decimos** / **dicen** ) la verdad.

2. Las hermanas ( **vienes** / **vienen** ) tarde.

3. Yo ( **viene** / **vengo** ) a tiempo.

4. Mis padres ( **sales** / **salen** ) del trabajo a las cinco.

5. Tú ( **dices** / **digo** ) que sabes más que yo.

**B.** Write the correct verb form to complete each sentence.

1. Mi profesor _____ (**decir**) que soy buen estudiante.

2. Yo _____ (**salir**) de casa muy temprano por la mañana.

3. Mis tíos _____ (**venir**) a mi casa esta noche.

4. Yo siempre _____ (**decir**) la verdad.

5. Nosotros _____ (**salir**) de la escuela a las tres y media.

6. La profesora está enferma y no _____ (**venir**) a clase hoy.

Write the Spanish vocabulary word below each picture. Be sure to include the article for each noun.

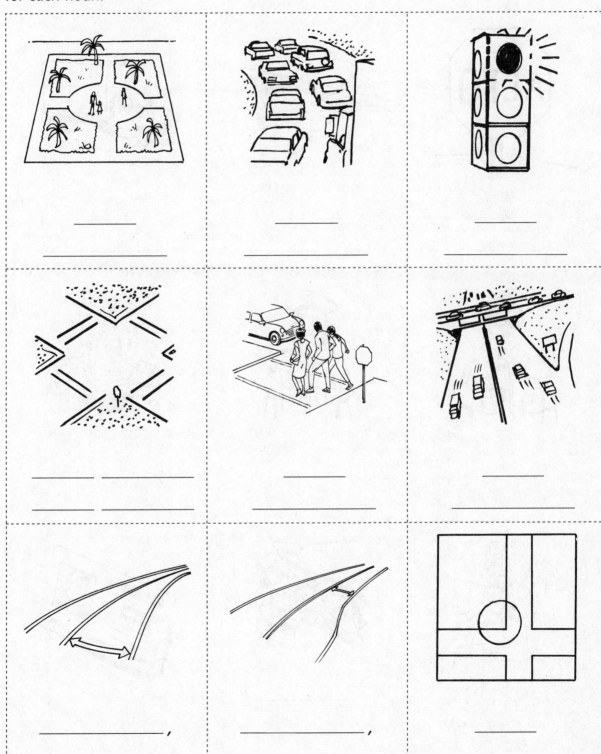

Write the Spanish vocabulary word or phrase below each picture. Be sure to include the article for each noun.

Write the Spanish vocabulary word below each picture. If there is a word or phrase, copy it in the space provided. Be sure to include the article for each noun.

| | | |
|---|---|---|
| _____ | _____ | **¡Basta!**<br><br>_____ |
| **De acuerdo.**<br><br>_____ | **dejar**<br><br>_____ | **Déjame en paz.**<br><br>_____ |
| **despacio**<br><br>_____ | **estar seguro, segura**<br><br>_____ , _____ | **Me estás poniendo nervioso, nerviosa.**<br><br>_____<br>_____<br>_____ , _____ |

Copy the word or phrase in the space provided. Be sure to include the article for each noun.

| | | |
|---|---|---|
| **peligroso, peligrosa**<br><br><br>_____ ,<br><br>_____ | **quitar**<br><br><br><br>_____ | **tener cuidado**<br><br><br><br>_____ |
| **ya**<br><br><br><br>_____ | **aproximadamente**<br><br><br><br>_____ | **¿Cómo se va...?**<br><br><br>_____<br><br>_____ |
| **complicado, complicada**<br><br><br>_____ ,<br><br>_____ | **cruzar**<br><br><br><br>_____ | **desde**<br><br><br><br>_____ |

**Capítulo 3B**

Copy the word or phrase in the space provided. Be sure to include the article for each noun.

| | | |
|---|---|---|
| **hasta** | **por** | **quedar** |
| _____ | _____ | _____ |
| **seguir** | **tener prisa** | **la avenida** |
| _____ | _____ | _____ |
| **la cuadra** | **en medio de** | **parar** |
| _____ | _____ | _____ |

Copy the word or phrase in the space provided. Be sure to include the article for each noun. These blank cards can be used to write and practice other Spanish vocabulary for the chapter.

| | | |
|---|---|---|
| **pasar** | **el conductor, la conductora** | **esperar** |
| _____ | _____ _____, _____ _____ | _____ |
| **manejar** | **el metro** | |
| _____ | _____ _____ | _____ |
| | | |
| _____ | _____ | _____ |

Tear out this page. Write the English words on the lines. Fold the paper along the dotted line to see the correct answers so you can check your work.

la avenida _____

el camión _____

la carretera _____

el conductor,
la conductora _____

el tráfico _____

el cruce de calles _____

la cuadra _____

la esquina _____

la estatua _____

la fuente _____

el peatón _____

el permiso
de manejar _____

la plaza _____

el policía, la policía _____

el puente _____

Fold In

Nombre _____

Hora _____

Fecha _____

Tear out this page. Write the Spanish words on the lines. Fold the paper along the dotted line to see the correct answers so you can check your work.

avenue _____

truck _____

highway _____

driver _____

traffic _____

intersection _____

block _____

corner _____

statue _____

fountain _____

pedestrian _____

driver's license _____

plaza _____

police officer _____

bridge _____

Fold In

Tear out this page. Write the English words on the lines. Fold the paper along the dotted line to see the correct answers so you can check your work.

ancho, ancha        _____

¡Basta!             _____

De acuerdo.         _____

dejar               _____

Déjame en paz.      _____

despacio            _____

esperar             _____

peligroso,          _____
peligrosa

tener cuidado       _____

ya                  _____

cruzar              _____

parar               _____

pasar               _____

quedar              _____

Fold In

**Capítulo 3B**   Fecha _____   **Vocabulary Check, Sheet 4**

Tear out this page. Write the Spanish words on the lines. Fold the paper along the dotted line to see the correct answers so you can check your work.

wide _____

Enough! _____

OK. Agreed. _____

to leave, to let _____

Leave me alone. _____

slowly _____

to wait _____

dangerous _____

to be careful _____

already _____

to cross _____

stop _____

to pass, to go _____

to be located _____

Fold In ←

# Direct object pronouns: *me, te, nos* (p. 166)

- Remember that you can replace a direct object noun with a direct object pronoun.
- The pronouns **lo, la, los,** and **las** can refer to people, places, or things. The pronouns **me, te, nos,** and **os** refer only to people, not to places or things.
- Here are all the direct object pronouns.

| Singular | | Plural | |
|---|---|---|---|
| **me** | me | **nos** | us |
| **te** | me *(familiar)* | **os** | you *(familiar)* |
| **lo** | it, him, you *(masculine formal)* | **los** | them, you *(masculine formal)* |
| **la** | it, her, you *(feminine formal)* | **las** | them, you *(feminine formal)* |

- Remember that in Spanish the subject and the verb ending tell who does the action. The direct object pronoun indicates who receives the action:

  **¿Me escuchas, por favor?**     *Can you listen to me please?*

**A.** Read the following sentences. In each sentence, circle the subject of the verb and underline the verb ending that matches the subject. Follow the model.

Modelo  (Lucas) te habl<u>ó</u> por teléfono anoche.

1. Lola me lleva a mí a la ciudad.

2. Nuestros amigos nos esperan allí.

3. Yo los busqué a Ricardo y a Enrique ayer.

4. Tú nos dices la verdad, pero tu hermano no.

5. Elena me ayuda a ir hasta la plaza.

6. La banda te sigue porque eres conductora.

**B.** Now, look again at the sentences from exercise A. This time, draw an arrow pointing to the direct object pronoun. Follow the model.

        ↓
Modelo  Lucas te habló por teléfono anoche.

1. Lola me lleva a mí a la ciudad.

2. Nuestros amigos nos esperan allí.

3. Yo los busqué a Ricardo y a Enrique ayer.

# Direct object pronouns (*continued*)

**4.** Tú nos dices la verdad, pero tu hermano no.

**5.** Elena me ayuda a ir hasta la plaza.

**6.** La banda te sigue porque eres conductora.

**C.** Read the questions below and circle the letter of the correct answer for each. Follow the model.

**Modelo**    Julio te ayuda a veces, ¿no?

        **(a.)** Sí, me ayuda mucho.       **b.** Sí, te ayuda mucho.

**1.** ¿Me esperas en la esquina cerca del museo?

    **a.** Sí, nos espera en la esquina.       **b.** Sí, te espero allí.

**2.** El policía siempre nos deja pasar, ¿verdad?

    **a.** No, a veces no nos deja pasar.       **b.** No, no nos dice la verdad.

**3.** ¿Te pongo nerviosa?

    **a.** Sí, me pones nerviosa.       **b.** Sí, me pongo nervioso.

**4.** ¿El policía me va a dejar en paz?

    **a.** No, no me pones una multa.       **b.** No, te va a poner una multa.

**5.** Señor policía, ¿me puede quitar la multa, por favor?

    **a.** Sí, me puede quitar la multa.       **b.** Sí, le puedo quitar la multa.

# Irregular affirmative *tú* commands (p. 168)

- Remember that to form an affirmative command in the **tú** form, use the **él/ella/ Ud.** form of the verb.

  **Habla** con la policía.        *Talk to the police.*

**A.** Write the affirmative **tú** command of the regular verbs in parentheses. Follow the model.

Modelo   (**manejar**) Patricia, ___*maneja*___ con cuidado, por favor.

1. (**esperar**) Tere, _____ un minuto, por favor.

2. (**escribir**) Ramón, _____ tu nombre aquí, por favor.

3. (**dejar**) Esteban, _____ el coche aquí, por favor.

4. (**leer**) Lisa, _____ el párrafo, por favor.

5. (**doblar**) Raúl, _____ a la derecha aquí.

- Some verbs have irregular forms for the affirmative **tú** commands. To form the command, take the **yo** form of the present tense and drop the ending **-go**.

| infinitive | yo form | command form | example |
|---|---|---|---|
| poner | pon**go** | **pon** | **Pon la mesa.** |
| tener | ten**go** | **ten** | **¡Ten cuidado!** |
| decir | di**go** | **di** | **¡Di la verdad!** |
| salir | sal**go** | **sal** | **Sal de la casa.** |
| venir | ven**go** | **ven** | **Ven acá, por favor.** |

**B.** Complete the following sentences with the **tú** command of the verb in parentheses. Follow the model.

Modelo   (**Salir**) ___*Sal*___ del coche sucio.

1. (**Tener**) _____ tu nuevo permiso de manejar.

2. ¡Miguel, (**venir**) _____ rápido; el tren va a salir!

3. (**Decir**) _____ tu nombre al policía.

4. (**Poner**) _____ el libro en la mesa.

5. (**Salir**) _____ a las doce para llegar a tiempo.

# Irregular affirmative *tú* commands (*continued*)

- The verbs **hacer, ser,** and **ir** also have irregular **tú** commands:

| hacer: **haz** | ser: **sé** | ir: **ve** |
|---|---|---|

**C.** Complete the following exchanges with the **tú** command of the verb in parentheses. Follow the model.

| Modelo | ELISA: ¿Cómo llego a la fiesta, Mamá? |
|---|---|

> MAMÁ: ¡(Ir) ____Ve____ en un coche!

1. CARLOS: No sé dónde queda la plaza. ¿Qué hago?

   MAMÁ: ¡(Hacer) _____ una pregunta!

2. PATTY: ¿Qué debo hacer para no recibir multas de la policía?

   RUTH: (Ser) _____ una buena conductora.

3. ALBERTO: ¿Cómo llego a la Avenida Juárez?

   LOLA: ¡(Ir) _____ en el metro!

4. JUANJO: Tengo miedo de hablar con la policía sobre la multa que recibí.

   RAÚL: (Ser) _____ cortés y todo va a estar bien.

- If you need to use an affirmative command with a direct object pronoun, the pronoun is attached to the end of the command. Remember to add a written accent over the stressed vowel if the command had two or more syllables.

  **Ponlo aquí.**          *Put it here.*

  **Búscame en el parque.**   *Look for me in the park.*

**D.** Read the sentences below. Complete the second sentence in each pair by writing the appropriate direct object pronoun in the space provided. Don't forget to add any necessary written accents.

| Modelo | Manda la carta. | Mánda _la_ . |
|---|---|---|

1. Haz la pregunta.              Haz_____.

2. Pide las direcciones.          Píde_____.

3. Visita el Parque de las Palomas.   Visíta_____.

4. Pon el permiso de manejar en tu mochila.   Pon_____ en tu mochila.

5. Mira las señales cuando manejas.   Míra_____.

6. Invita a tu amigo y a mí a la fiesta.   Invíta_____ a la fiesta.

# Present progressive: irregular forms (p. 171)

- Remember that you form the present progressive by using **estar** + the present participle:

  **Estoy hablando con Lucía.**   *I am talking to Lucía.*

**A.** Fill in the blanks using **estar** + the present participle of the verbs in parentheses. The first one is done for you.

1. (**hablar**) Mis padres _____están_____ _____hablando_____ con la policía.

2. (**compartir**) Juanita y Pepito _____ _____ la comida.

3. (**quedar**) Yo me _____ _____ en el hotel.

4. (**poner**) Tú me _____ _____ nerviosa.

5. (**doblar**) El coche _____ _____ en la esquina.

- Some verbs have irregular present participle forms. To form the present participle of -**ir** stem-changing verbs, the **e** in the stem of the infinitive changes to **i**, and then the **o** in the stem changes to **u**:

| decir → **diciendo** | pedir → **pidiendo** | repetir → **repitiendo** |
|---|---|---|
| servir → **sirviendo** | seguir → **siguiendo** | dormir → **durmiendo** |

**B.** Fill in the missing vowels to form the present participle of the verbs that have been started in each sentence below. Follow the model.

**Modelo**   La camarera está s_i_rv_i_ _e_ndo a las chicas primero.

1. El perro está d__rm__ __ndo en el piso.

2. Mi mamá me está s__gu__ __ndo en su coche.

3. La profesora está rep__t__ __ndo la tarea.

- To form the present participle of the following -**er** verbs, add -**yendo** instead of -**iendo**:

| creer → **creyendo** | leer → **leyendo** | traer → **trayendo** |
|---|---|---|

**C.** Write the present participle of each verb in parentheses to complete the sentence. The first one has been done for you.

1. Yo estoy _____creyendo_____ en mi equipo. (**creer**)

2. Los estudiantes están _____ sus tareas. (**traer**)

3. Nosotras estamos _____ un libro. (**leer**)

4. Mario está _____ la comida. (**traer**)

# Present progressive: irregular forms (*continued*)

**D.** Change the underlined verb in the following sentences from the present tense to the present progressive tense. Follow the model.

**Modelo** Adriana <u>dice</u> la verdad.     <u>está</u>     <u>diciendo</u>

1. Tú <u>pides</u> ayuda.     _____ _____

2. Mi padre <u>lee</u> el periódico.     _____ _____

3. La profesora <u>repite</u> la pregunta.     _____ _____

4. Ana y yo <u>traemos</u> las bebidas.     _____ _____

5. El camarero <u>sirve</u> la comida.     _____ _____

6. Paulo y Javier <u>duermen</u> en clase.     _____ _____

7. Los estudintes <u>siguen</u> al profesor.     _____ _____

8. Yo no te <u>creo</u>.     _____ _____

• When you use a direct object pronoun with a present progressive verb, the pronoun can either come before **estar** or attached to the present participle. It is necessary to add a written accent if the pronoun is attached to the present participle.

    **Lara lo está trayendo.**    *or*    **Lara está trayéndolo.**

**E.** Rewrite the sentences adding the direct object pronoun to the end of the present progressive form. Remember to write an accent on the stressed **a** or **e**. Follow the model.

**Modelo** Felipe nos está llevando.     *Felipe está llevándonos* .

1. Nosotros lo estamos esperando. _____ .

2. Ella me está siguiendo. _____ .

3. Tú las estás leyendo. _____ .

4. Sancho me está diciendo la verdad. _____ .

5. El profesor nos está enseñando. _____ .

## Lectura: Guía del buen conductor (pp. 174–175)

**A.** The reading in your textbook is about developing safe driving habits. You may not understand the meaning of some important words in the reading. Sometimes you can use context clues to guess the meaning of these unknown words. Read the following sentences and answer the questions.

> *Manejar bien requiere muchos años de práctica. Si puedes practicar todos los días después de obtener tu permiso de manejar de estudiante, es mejor porque así vas adquiriendo experiencia.*

**1.** In the first sentence, what words tell you what **requiere** means?

_____

**2.** What do you think **vas adquiriendo experiencia** means? How do you know? (Hint: Do any of these words look or sound like English?)

_____

**B.** This excerpt is taken from the first section of your textbook reading. Read the excerpt and find the meaning of the underlined words below by using context clues. Circle the choice that best describes the meaning of each word.

> *Guía del buen conductor*
> *Un buen conductor siempre debe estar <u>alerta</u> para evitar accidentes. No es difícil: simplemente tienes que estar atento...*
>
> *Conductores agresivos*
> *Si el conductor es muy agresivo, puedes <u>reportarlo</u> con la policía.*

**1.** alerta:

  **a.** atento

  **b.** aburrido

**2.** reportar:

  **a.** hacer una pregunta

  **b.** informar

**C.** Imagine that you are driving a car. You want to reassure your passenger that you have safe driving habits. Circle the word in parentheses that best completes each sentence.

**1.** Estoy ( **manejando** / **vistiendo** ) con atención.

**2.** La carretera es estrecha, por eso estoy ( **siguiendo** / **poniendo** ) mucha atención.

**3.** No estoy ( **diciendo** / **leyendo** ) en el coche.

**4.** No estoy ( **manejando** / **durmiendo** ).

**5.** Estoy ( **siguiendo** / **durmiendo** ) las señales de tráfico.

# Presentación escrita (p. 177)

**Task:** Pretend that you have received your first driver's license. Make a poster that reminds your classmates of safe driving practices and important traffic signs.

**A.** Look at the traffic signs below. Then, write the meaning of each sign in English in the middle column and in Spanish in the right column.

| | English | Spanish |
|---|---|---|
| 1. ALTO | | |
| 2. (no right turn) | | |
| 3. (pedestrian) | | |

**B.** From the following list, circle the word describing the meaning of each traffic light color.

rojo ( **seguir / parar** )

amarillo ( **parar / manejar** )

verde ( **seguir / parar** )

**C.** The following are two actions a driver should take to drive safely. Think about two other actions for safe driving which you have read about in the chapter. Then write them below.

1. manejar despacio por calles estrechas
2. tener cuidado cerca de las señales de tráfico
3. _____
4. _____

**D.** Read through your answers in **parts A, B,** and **C.** Decide which information to use to make a poster about safe driving practices. Be sure to include drawings or photos of traffic signs and some of the safe driving practices.

**E.** Share your poster with a partner who will check the following:

_____ Does the poster present important and accurate information?

_____ Is the visual representation clear and easy to understand?

_____ Is there anything to add, change, or correct?

# A ver si recuerdas: Suffixes (p. 183)

- To say that something is *small* or *little* or to add a feeling of affection to a noun, use the suffix **-ito** (**-a, -os, -as**). This is called the diminutive. Generally, you drop the **-o, -a, -os,** or **-as** from the end of the noun and add the suffix.

   **perro → perrito**      **novela → novelita**

**A.** Change these nouns to the diminutive. First, drop the underlined part of the noun. Then, add the appropriate suffix: **-ito, -ita, -itos, -itas.** Follow the model.

   **Modelo**   libro        *librito*  _____

   **1.** escuela      _____

   **2.** hermanos     _____

   **3.** gato         _____

   **4.** abuelo       _____

   **5.** zapatos      _____

   **6.** vaso         _____

   **7.** galletas     _____

   **8.** regalo       _____

- To add emphasis to an adjective (as if adding *really* in English), use the suffix **-ísimo** (**-a, -os, -as**). Remember the written accent over the first "i" of the suffix.

   **Mi amiga es divertida.**        *My friend is fun.*
   **Mi amiga es divertidísima.**     *My friend is really fun.*

**B.** Rewrite the descriptions of the people and things in these sentences, using the **-ísimo** form of the adjective. Follow the model.

   **Modelo**   Julia es muy inteligente.        *Es inteligentísima* _____.

   **1.** La fiesta fue muy buena.      _____.

   **2.** Estas piñatas son muy lindas.      _____.

   **3.** Los globos son preciosos.      _____.

   **4.** Mi mamá estuvo muy ocupada hoy.  _____.

   **5.** Las fotos son muy graciosas.      _____.

Nombre _____     Hora _____

**Capítulo 4A**      Fecha _____     **Vocabulary Flash Cards, Sheet 1**

Write the Spanish vocabulary word or phrase below each picture. Be sure to include the article for each noun.

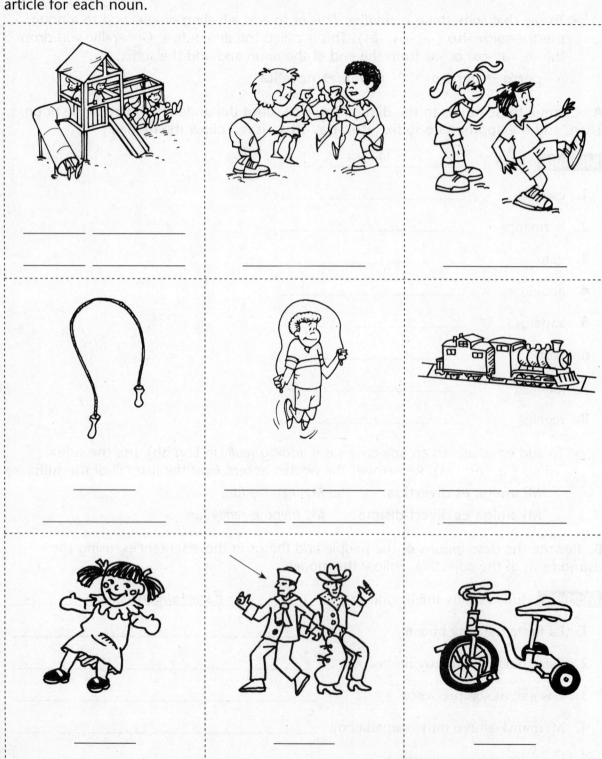

Write the Spanish vocabulary word below each picture. If there is a word or phrase, copy it in the space provided. Be sure to include the article for each noun.

de niño,
de niña

Copy the word or phrase in the space provided. Be sure to include the article for each noun.

| | | |
|---|---|---|
| **de vez en cuando** | **mentir** | **obedecer** |
| _____ <br> _____ | _____ | _____ |
| **ofrecer** | **permitir** | **por lo general** |
| _____ | _____ | _____ _____ <br> _____ |
| **todo el mundo** | **de pequeño, de pequeña** | **la verdad** |
| _____ <br> _____ _____ | _____ _____ , <br> _____ _____ | _____ <br> _____ |

**Capítulo 4A**   Fecha _____   **Vocabulary Flash Cards, Sheet 4**

Copy the word or phrase in the space provided. Be sure to include the article for each noun.

| | | |
|---|---|---|
| **consentido, consentida**<br><br><br>_____, <br>_____ | **desobediente**<br><br><br>_____ | **generoso, generosa**<br><br><br>_____, <br>_____ |
| **obediente**<br><br><br>_____ | **tímido, tímida**<br><br><br>_____, <br>_____ | **travieso, traviesa**<br><br><br>_____, <br>_____ |
| **coleccionar**<br><br><br>_____ | **el mundo**<br><br><br>_____ | **portarse bien/mal**<br><br><br>_____ |

These blank cards can be used to write and practice other Spanish vocabulary for the chapter.

_____     _____     _____

_____     _____     _____

_____     _____     _____

Tear out this page. Write the English words on the lines. Fold the paper along the dotted line to see the correct answers so you can check your work.

los bloques _____

la colección _____

la cuerda _____

el dinosaurio _____

la muñeca _____

el muñeco _____

el oso de peluche _____

el tren eléctrico _____

el triciclo _____

el pez _____

la tortuga _____

la guardería infantil _____

el patio de recreo _____

el vecino, la vecina _____

Fold In

**Capítulo 4A**    Fecha _____   **Vocabulary Check, Sheet 2**

Tear out this page. Write the Spanish words on the lines. Fold the paper along the dotted line to see the correct answers so you can check your work.

blocks _____

collection _____

rope _____

dinosaur _____

doll _____

action figure _____

teddy bear _____

electric train _____

tricycle _____

fish _____

turtle _____

daycare center _____

playground _____

neighbor _____

Fold In ←

Tear out this page. Write the English words on the lines. Fold the paper along the dotted line to see the correct answers so you can check your work.

coleccionar _____

molestar _____

pelearse _____

saltar (a la cuerda) _____

mentir _____

obedecer _____

permitir _____

portarse
bien/mal _____

de niño, de niña _____

de vez en cuando _____

Fold In

**Capítulo 4A**   Fecha _____   **Vocabulary Check, Sheet 4**

Tear out this page. Write the Spanish words on the lines. Fold the paper along the dotted line to see the correct answers so you can check your work.

to collect          _____

to bother           _____

to fight            _____

to jump (rope)      _____

to lie              _____

to obey             _____

to permit, to allow _____

to behave
well/badly          _____

as a child          _____

once in a while     _____

Fold In

# The imperfect tense: Regular verbs (p. 194)

- The imperfect tense is used to talk about actions that happened repeatedly in the past.

    **Rafael caminaba y Ramiro corría en el parque.**
    *Rafael used to walk and Ramiro used to run in the park.*

- Here are the regular forms of **-ar, -er,** and **-ir** verbs in the imperfect tense:

| | jugar | hacer | vivir |
|---|---|---|---|
| yo | jug**aba** | hac**ía** | viv**ía** |
| tú | jug**abas** | hac**ías** | viv**ías** |
| usted/él/ella | jug**aba** | hac**ía** | viv**ía** |
| nosotros/nosotras | jug**ábamos** | hac**íamos** | viv**íamos** |
| vosotros/vosotras | jug**abais** | hac**íais** | viv**íais** |
| ustedes/ellos/ellas | jug**aban** | hac**ían** | viv**ían** |

- Note the accents on **jugábamos** and throughout the conjugations of the **-er** and **-ir** verbs.

- These expressions can cue you to use the imperfect: **generalmente, por lo general, a menudo, muchas veces, de vez en cuando, todos los días, nunca.**

**A.** Write the infinitive form of each conjugated verb. The first one is done for you.

1. jugaba _____*jugar*_____     5. ofrecía _____

2. molestaba _____     6. permitían _____

3. coleccionaban _____     7. corríamos _____

4. obedecías _____     8. vivíamos _____

**B.** Fill in the blanks with the correct form of the **-ar** verbs in the imperfect tense. Follow the model.

**Modelo**  Tú habl_*abas*_ con mucha gente.

1. Alicia siempre molest_____ a su hermana.

2. Mis tíos nunca nos regal_____ nada a nosotros.

3. Pedro le d_____ agua al perro muchas veces.

4. Yo siempre me port_____ bien enfrente de mis padres.

5. A menudo nosotros jug_____ en el parque.

# The imperfect tense: regular verbs (*continued*)

**C.** Write the correct endings for the **-er** and **-ir** verbs below. Follow the model.

**Modelo** Por lo general, yo obedec_ía___ a mis padres.

1. Mis primos me ofrec_____ sus bloques de vez en cuando.

2. A menudo mis tíos me permit_____ comer una galletas.

3. Generalmente, mamá pon_____ la mesa.

4. Mis hermanos y yo hac_____ la cama todos los días.

5. Tú viv_____ en la misma ciudad que yo.

**D.** Complete the sentences below to describe what people *used to do*. Use the drawings and the verbs in parentheses as clues. Follow the model.

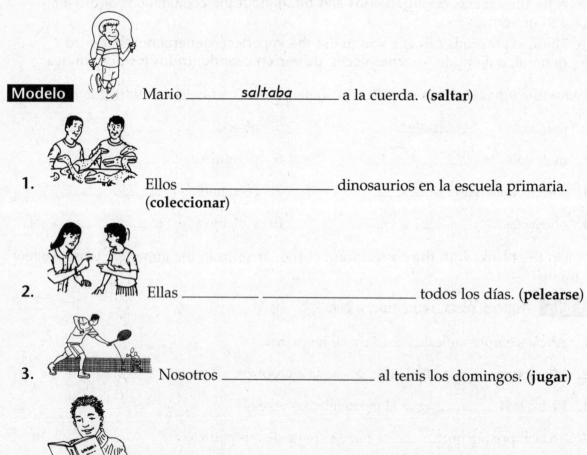

**Modelo** Mario _____saltaba_____ a la cuerda. (**saltar**)

1. Ellos _____ dinosaurios en la escuela primaria. (**coleccionar**)

2. Ellas _____ _____ todos los días. (**pelearse**)

3. Nosotros _____ al tenis los domingos. (**jugar**)

4. Tú _____ en la biblioteca los fines de semana. (**leer**)

# The imperfect tense: irregular verbs (p. 196)

- There are only three irregular verbs in the imperfect tense: **ir**, **ser**, and **ver**. Here are their forms:

|  | ir | ser | ver |
|---|---|---|---|
| yo | iba | era | veía |
| tú | ibas | eras | veías |
| usted/él/ella | iba | era | veía |
| nosotros/nosotras | íbamos | éramos | veíamos |
| vosotros/vosotras | ibais | erais | veíais |
| ustedes/ellos/ellas | iban | eran | veían |

- Note that only the **nosotros** forms of **ir** and **ser** carry accents.
- **Ver** uses the exact same endings as regular -er verbs, and is only irregular because of the added "**e**".

**A.** Choose the correct verb in parentheses to complete each sentence. Circle your choice. Use the chart above to help you. Follow the model.

**Modelo**   Clara y Nubia ( (**eran**) / **iban** ) mis amigas.

1. Por lo general, yo ( **era** / **veía** ) a mis primas.

2. Mis primos nunca ( **veían** / **iban** ) conmigo al mercado.

3. Mis hermanos y yo ( **éramos** / **íbamos** ) muy traviesos.

4. ¿Tú ( **ibas** / **veías** ) muchas películas?

**B.** Complete the following sentences using the imperfect form of the verb in parentheses. Follow the model.

**Modelo**   Nosotros (**ir**) _____ *íbamos* _____ a la escuela todos los días.

1. ¡Mi mamá (**ser**) _____ muy traviesa de niña!

2. Nosotros generalmente (**ver**) _____ la tele en casa.

3. De niña, yo (**ir**) _____ a la casa de mis tíos de vez en cuando.

4. La familia de mi mamá (**ver**) _____ a la abuela durante las vacaciones.

5. Juana y yo (**ser**) _____ muy buenas amigas.

**Capítulo 4A**

# The imperfect tense: review

**A.** Below are two paragraphs about Christopher Columbus. As you read, fill in the blanks with the appropriate imperfect form of the verbs given. The first one has been done for you.

Cuando Cristóbal Colón _____*tenía*_____ **(tener)** diez años, le

_____ **(gustar)** mucho navegar (*to sail*) con su papá. Cristóbal y

sus amigos _____ **(imaginar)** lugares distantes y exóticos que

ellos _____ **(ir)** a visitar algún día. Sus padres siempre

_____ **(decir)**: "Es importante imaginar y descubrir (*discover*)".

Cristóbal _____ **(pensar)** mucho y realmente

_____ **(querer)** buscar un lugar nuevo.

Cuando _____ **(ser)** mayor, él _____ **(hablar)** de

vez en cuando con los reyes (*kings, rulers*) de España para pedirles dinero

para sus exploraciones. Los reyes _____ **(decir)**: " Cristóbal, tú

_____ **(ser)** un buen explorador de niño con tu padre. Tú

_____ **(ver)** muchos lugares nuevos. Es importante ahora

descubrir una nueva ruta a la India". Cristóbal siempre _____

**(explorar)** y _____ **(ver)** muchos lugares nuevos, pero nunca

encontró la ruta a la India.

# Indirect object pronouns (p. 199)

- An indirect object tells *to whom* or *for whom* something is done.

  **Julio escribió una carta a Susana.**   *Julio wrote a letter to Susana.*

- Indirect object pronouns can replace an indirect object.

  **Julio le escribió una carta.**   *Julio wrote her a letter.*

- Indirect object pronouns, especially **le** and **les**, can also be used with an indirect object.

  **Julio le escribió una carta a Susana.**   *Julio wrote a letter to Susana (to her).*

- Here are the forms of the indirect object pronouns:

| Singular | Plural |
|---|---|
| **me**  (to/for) me | **nos**  (to/for) us |
| **te**  (to/for) you *(familiar)* | **os**  (to/for) you *(familiar)* |
| **le**  (to/for) him, her, you *(formal)* | **les**  (to/for) them, you *(formal)* |

**A.** Circle the indirect object pronoun in each sentence. Follow the model.

**Modelo**   Tú (le) escribías cartas a tu amigo boliviano Carlos.

1. Yo le pedía a mamá una muñeca.

2. Mi abuela me daba muchos besos.

3. Carlos y yo le ofrecíamos unos chocolates.

4. Claudia nos iba a comprar ropa.

5. Roberto les ofrecía el triciclo a sus hermanas.

**B.** Circle the appropriate indirect object pronoun in parentheses to complete each sentence. Then, underline the part of the sentence that indicates *to whom* the pronoun refers. The first one is done for you.

1. Generalmente mi abuela ((nos)/ me ) compraba muchos juguetes a <u>nosotros</u>.

2. Mamá y yo siempre ( le / nos ) dábamos tarjetas bonitas a la tía.

3. Yo ( te / le ) ofrecía dulces a ti en la escuela primaria.

4. Tú siempre ( les / te ) dabas osos de peluche a mis hermanas.

5. Mis padres no ( me / les ) permitían a mí llevar gorra a la iglesia.

**Capítulo 4A**   Fecha _____

# Indirect object pronouns (*continued*)

**C.** Look at each of the following sentences. First, underline the indirect object noun. Then, in the space provided, put the indirect object pronoun that corresponds to the noun you underlined. Follow the model.

**Modelo**   Nuestros padres siempre ___*nos*___ decían la verdad a <u>nosotros</u>.

1. Por lo general, mis amigos _____ prestaban a mí sus juguetes.

2. Los abuelos de Alicia siempre _____ querían dar a ella buenas cosas.

3. La profesora _____ permitía a los estudiantes jugar en el patio de recreo.

4. Yo no _____ daba dinero a ti para ver las películas.

5. Tío Leo _____ compraba a mi hermano las vías (*tracks*) para su tren eléctrico.

> • Indirect object pronouns can be placed before the verb or attached to the infinitive.
>
>   **Mi abuela nunca *me* quería dar dinero en mi cumpleaños.**
>   **Mi abuela nunca quería dar*me* dinero en mi cumpleaños.**

**D.** Look at the sentences below and write a new sentence with the same meaning, placing the indirect object pronoun differently. Follow the model.

**Modelo**   Tía Lisa me quería llevar a la guardería infantil.

*Tía Lisa quería llevarme a la guardería infantil* _____.

1. Yo no les podía mentir a mis padres.

   _____ .

2. Los tíos siempre nos tenían que decir que éramos niños traviesos.

   _____ .

3. Mis primos malos siempre me querían molestar.

   _____ .

4. A veces mis hermanos y yo no les queríamos obedecer a nuestros padres.

   _____ .

## Lectura: El grillo y el jaguar (pp. 202–203)

> Making predictions is a useful strategy to help prepare you for a reading.

**A.** The reading in your textbook is a fable from Mexico. Look at the title of the reading and the pictures. Then, using the fables you know as guides, like *Aesop's Fables,* list three things that you think might happen in this fable.

1. _____

2. _____

3. _____

**B.** In the following paragraph from the reading, the jaguar challenges the cricket to a race. Read the paragraph and then circle the option below that describes what you think will happen.

> —Vamos a hacer una carrera *(race)* hasta aquella roca enorme que está por donde empiezan las montañas. Si llegas primero, te perdono todo y puedes seguir cantando, pero si llego primero yo, te prohíbo cantar.

1. The cricket wins the race and can continue singing.
2. The jaguar wins the race and the cricket can't sing.

**C.** After you have read *El grillo y el jaguar,* write the letter of the answer that best completes each sentence.

1. Los personajes principales *(main characters)* de esta fábula son: _____
   a. el grillo y el jaguar
   b. el jaguar y el jardín
   c. el grillo y el lago

2. El problema de esta fábula es: _____
   a. El grillo quiere correr tan rápidamente como el jaguar.
   b. El jaguar quiere cantar.
   c. Al jaguar no le gusta la canción del grillo.

3. La moraleja *(moral)* de esta fábula es: _____
   a. El grillo gana porque corre más rápidamente.
   b. El grillo gana porque el jaguar es simpático.
   c. El grillo gana porque es más inteligente.

# Presentación oral (p. 205)

**Task:** Describe what you were like when you were a small child and draw a series of pictures that illustrate your sentences.

**A.** Think about what you were like when you were a small child, what things you used to do, and what things you weren't allowed to do. Then, complete the following sentences.

1. Cuando era niño(a), era _____ y _____.

2. Yo jugaba con _____.

3. Me gustaba jugar _____.

4. Yo tenía que _____.

5. Mis padres no me permitían _____.

**B.** On a separate sheet of paper, make a drawing or cut out pictures from a magazine to illustrate each of your sentences from **part A**. Number your pictures 1 to 5.

**C.** Use your sentences from **part A** and your drawings from **part B** to prepare your presentation. You can practice your presentation with a partner. Make sure that:

- your sentences describe the pictures in order
- you use complete sentences
- you speak clearly so that you can be understood

**D.** Now, talk about what you were like when you were a child. Hold up your pictures in order during the presentation as you say your sentences to describe them. You can follow the model.

> *Cuando era niño(a), yo era obediente. Yo jugaba con mis amigos. Me gustaba jugar con mi triciclo. Yo tenía que portarme bien. Mis padres no me permitían saltar en la cama.*

**E.** Your teacher will probably grade you on the following:

- the amount of information you communicate
- how easy it is to understand you
- the quality of visuals

## Capítulo 4B

Fecha _____  **Vocabulary Flash Cards, Sheet 1**

Write the Spanish vocabulary word or phrase below each picture. Be sure to include the article for each noun.

_____

_____

_____

_____

_____

_____

_____

_____

_____

Nombre _____     Hora _____

**Capítulo 4B**     Fecha _____     **Vocabulary Flash Cards, Sheet 2**

Write the Spanish vocabulary word or phrase below each picture. Be sure to include the article for each noun.

_____

_____

_____

_____

_____

_____

_____

_____

_____

Write the Spanish vocabulary word below each picture. If there is a word or phrase, copy it in the space provided. Be sure to include the article for each noun.

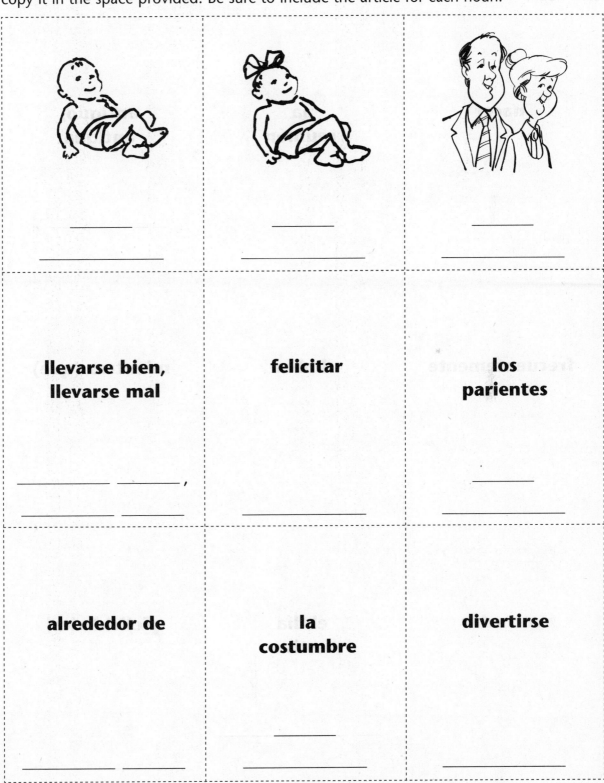

| | | |
|---|---|---|
| _____ _____ | _____ | _____ |
| **llevarse bien, llevarse mal** | **felicitar** | **los parientes** |
| _____ _____, | _____ | _____ |
| **alrededor de** | **la costumbre** | **divertirse** |
| _____ | _____ | _____ |

Copy the word or phrase in the space provided. Be sure to include the article for each noun.

| | | |
|---|---|---|
| **nacer** | **la reunión** | **antiguo, antigua** |
| | | |
| _____ | _____ | _____, _____ |
| **frecuentemente** | **había** | **mientras (que)** |
| | | |
| _____ | _____ | _____ |
| **recordar** | **el día festivo** | **¡Felicidades!** |
| | | |
| _____ | ____ ____ | _____ |

Tear out this page. Write the English words on the lines. Fold the paper along the dotted line to see the correct answers so you can check your work.

el bebé, la bebé          _____

el aniversario             _____

la costumbre               _____

el desfile                 _____

el día festivo             _____

la fiesta de
sorpresa                   _____

los fuegos
artificiales               _____

la reunión                 _____

los mayores                _____

los modales                _____

abrazar(se)                _____

besar(se)                  _____

dar(se) la mano            _____

Fold In

Tear out this page. Write the Spanish words on the lines. Fold the paper along the dotted line to see the correct answers so you can check your work.

baby                    _____

anniversary             _____

custom                  _____

parade                  _____

holiday                 _____

surprise party          _____

fireworks               _____

gathering               _____

grown-ups               _____

manners                 _____

to hug                  _____

to kiss                 _____

to shake hands          _____

Fold In

Tear out this page. Write the English words on the lines. Fold the paper along the dotted line to see the correct answers so you can check your work.

despedirse (de)    _____

saludar(se)    _____

sonreír    _____

contar (chistes)    _____

llorar    _____

reírse    _____

reunirse    _____

casarse (con)    _____

charlar    _____

cumplir años    _____

hacer un picnic    _____

nacer    _____

regalar    _____

recordar    _____

Fold In

Tear out this page. Write the Spanish words on the lines. Fold the paper along the dotted line to see the correct answers so you can check your work.

to say goodbye (to)  _____

to greet  _____

to smile  _____

to tell (jokes)  _____

to cry  _____

to laugh  _____

to meet  _____

to get married (to)  _____

to chat  _____

to have a birthday  _____

to have a picnic  _____

to be born  _____

to give (a gift)  _____

to remember  _____

Fold In

# The imperfect tense: describing a situation (p. 219)

- The imperfect tense is also used to describe people, places, and situations in the past:

   **La casa de mis abuelos era pequeña. Tenía dos dormitorios.**
   *My grandparents' house was small. It had two bedrooms.*

   **Mi abuelo era muy generoso.**
   *My grandfather was very generous.*

   **Las fiestas en la casa de mis abuelos eran muy divertidas.**
   *The parties at my grandparents' house were a lot of fun.*

**A.** Read the following paragraph and draw a line underneath all the verbs used to describe the situation. The first one has been done for you.

Cuando <u>era</u> niño, mi familia y yo siempre íbamos al lago. Mis abuelos tenían una

casa de verano que estaba cerca del lago. El lago era muy grande y bonito. Había

árboles alrededor del lago. Generalmente hacía mucho calor y por eso nos gustaba

nadar en el lago porque era más fresco (cool).

**B.** Read the following sentences about the paragraph in exercise A. Write **cierto** if they are true or **falso** if they are false. The first one is done for you.

1. La familia siempre iba al océano durante el verano. _____*falso*_____

2. Los tíos tenían una casa de verano cerca del lago. _____

3. Era un lago grande con árboles alrededor. _____

4. Hacía mucho calor en el verano. _____

5. No podían nadar en el lago. _____

# The imperfect tense (*continued*)

**C.** Complete the following sentences by writing the correct form of the verbs in parentheses using the imperfect tense. Use the the pictures to help you with the meaning of the sentences. Follow the model.

**Modelo**   El tío Pepe (**contar**) _____*contaba*_____ chistes.

1.   Nosotros (**charlar**) _____ con los parientes.

2.   Mis padres (**hacer**) _____ picnics.

3.   Yo (**pasar**) _____ tiempo con mis amigos.

4.   Mis hermanos (**jugar**) _____ al fútbol.

5.   Andréa (**tener**) _____ buenos modales.

6.   Tú (**divertirse**) _____ en las fiestas.

# The imperfect tense (*continued*)

- The imperfect is also used to talk about a past action or situation when no beginning or ending time is mentioned.

  **Había mucha gente en la fiesta para el aniversario de mis padres.**
  *There were many people at the party for my parents' anniversary.*

**D.** Look at the scene to start thinking about what is happening. Then, read the paragraph below it and fill in the missing form of the verbs in parentheses that describe the situation in the past. The first one is done for you.

Cuando yo __era__ (**ser**) niña, mis parientes _____ _____ (**reunirse**)

los domingos en casa de mi abuela. Mi abuela _____ (**preparar**) mucha

comida y mi madre y mis tías la _____ (**ayudar**). Yo

_____ (**jugar**) con mis primos. Todos nosotros (**llevarse**) _____

_____ muy bien, y _____ _____ (**divertirse**) mucho.

Nosotros _____ (**almorzar**) juntos (*together*) y _____

_____ (**reírse**) mucho contando chistes todo el tiempo.

# The imperfect tense (*continued*)

- The imperfect tense is also used to tell what someone was doing when something else happened (preterite):

  **Mis parientes *charlaban* cuando mi mamá *entró*.**
  *My relatives were chatting when my mother came in.*

**E.** Read the sentences below about a party. Circle the action that was taking place in the description. Then, underline the action that stopped it. The first one is done for you.

1. Yo (hablaba por teléfono) cuando <u>la fiesta empezó</u>.

2. Mis parientes y yo charlábamos cuando la fiesta empezó.

3. Cuando llegaron sus padres Luz contaba chistes.

4. Marta comía un pastel cuando le dieron los regalos.

5. La bebé jugaba cuando su abuela entró.

6. Cuando llegó Ana los primos bebían refrescos.

7. Luisa y Mariana bailaban cuando la fiesta terminó.

8. Cuando se fueron todos yo escribía sobre la fiesta.

9. Tú sacabas la basura cuando volvieron tus primos para celebrar más.

10. Cuando los primos y yo nos reunimos en el sótano, tú llamabas a la policía.

## The imperfect tense (*continued*)

**F.** Look at the drawing below of a surprise 50th anniversary party. Then, read the paragraph and fill in the blanks with the correct form of the verbs in parentheses using the imperfect tense. The first one is done for you.

La semana pasada ___*era*___ (**ser**) el aniversario de mis abuelos. Todos nuestros

parientes _____ (**estar**) en la casa de mis tíos. Las mujeres

_____ (**charlar**) y los hombres _____ (**contar**) chistes.

_____ (**Haber**) un pastel muy grande en la mesa. El pastel

_____ (**tener**) flores muy bonitas. Nosotros _____ _____

(**divertirse**) mucho.

**G.** Now, read the paragraph that tells what happened when the couple entered in the room. Fill in the blanks with the correct form of the verbs in parentheses using the preterite tense. The first one is done for you.

Cuando mis abuelos ___*llegaron*___ (**llegar**) todos les _____

(**felicitar**) a ellos. Las personas que charlaban antes, ahora _____

(**saludar**) a los abuelos, y algunas personas los _____ (**besar**).

Mamá _____ (**sacar**) los regalos de otro cuarto. Mis abuelos

_____ (**entrar**) y luego la fiesta _____ (**empezar**).

Nombre _____     Hora _____

**Capítulo 4B**     Fecha _____

# Reciprocal actions (p. 224)

- You can use **se** and **nos** to express the idea "(to) each other":

    **Luis y Jorge se veían con frecuencia.**
    *Luis and Jorge used to see each other frequently.*

    **Mis primos y yo nos escribíamos a menudo.**
    *My cousins and I used to write each other often.*

**A.** Choose the correct reciprocal verb to describe each picture. Then, write the correct form of the verb using the imperfect tense in the blank. Follow the model.

**Modelo**     Elena y María __*se*__ __*pelean*__. (pelearse / besarse)

1.     Alicia y yo _____ _____. (saludarse / besarse)

2.     Gregorio y Andrés _____ _____.
       **(darse la mano / abrazarse)**

3.     Daniel y Susi _____ _____ de Tomás.
       **(pelearse / despedirse)**

4.     Gloria y yo _____ _____. (saludarse / darse la mano)

5.     Antonio y Clara _____ _____. (abrazarse / verse)

## Lectura: El seis de enero (pp. 228–229)

**A.** *El seis de enero,* or Three King's Day, is one of the most beloved holidays for children in the Hispanic world. Before this holiday arrives, children write letters to the **Reyes Magos** (Three Kings or Wise Men), just as many children in the U.S. write to Santa Claus before Christmas. Put an X next to the things you would expect to find in a letter to the **Reyes Magos.**

1. Los niños dicen sus nombres.                          _____

2. Los niños dicen que se portan bien.              _____

3. Los niños dicen que se portan mal.               _____

4. Los niños dicen qué juguetes quieren.         _____

**B.** Now, read the following letter to the **Reyes Magos.** Answer the questions that follow.

> *4 de enero*
>
> *Queridos Reyes:*
>
> *Yo soy Carolina y quiero decirles que me porto bien con mami, papi y la maestra. Les escribo para pedirles una bicicleta rosada. Muchas gracias. Feliz año nuevo.*
>
> *Les quiere,*
>
> *Carolina*

1. See if you can find in the letter any of the things that you marked in **part A.** List three of them in English.

   _____ , _____ , _____

2. ¿Qué regalo pide Carolina? _____

3. ¿De qué color es la bicicleta? _____

**C.** Imagine that you are writing a letter to the **Reyes Magos** or to Santa Claus. Write about two gifts that you would like to have and tell why you want each one. You may follow the model.

Yo quiero _____ y _____ .

Yo quiero _____ porque _____ .

Yo quiero _____ porque _____ .

# Presentación escrita (p. 231)

**Task:** Some friends want to learn more about your favorite celebration or holiday. Write a brief paragraph describing such an event from your childhood.

**A.** Read the names of the following celebrations. Then, circle three of your favorite celebrations.

| ¿Qué celebrabas con tu familia? | | | |
|---|---|---|---|
| El Día de San Valentín | El Día de la Madre | La Navidad (*Christmas*) | La Semana Santa (*Easter week*) |
| El Año Nuevo | Halloween | El Día del Padre | El Día de Acción de Gracias |

**B.** Which of the celebrations or holidays from **part A** was your favorite when you were younger? Why was this your favorite celebration or holiday? Name the celebration and then give two reasons below.

_____ era mi celebración favorita porque _____

y _____

**C.** Use the chart below to think about what happened during your favorite celebration. What did you use to do? Where did you get together? Who was there? Circle all the expressions that describe the celebration.

| ¿Qué hacían? | ¿Dónde se reunían? | ¿Quiénes estaban? |
|---|---|---|
| bailábamos<br>había muchos regalos<br>comíamos mucho | en nuestra casa<br>en casa de los abuelos<br>en casa de mis tíos | mis primos y parientes<br>los amigos<br>muchos niños |

**D.** Now, write a brief paragraph about your favorite celebration or holiday. Use your answers from **parts B** and **C**. You may also follow the model below. Remember to use the imperfect in your description.

> *El Día de los Reyes Magos era mi celebración favorita porque lo celebraba con mi familia. Nosotros íbamos a la casa de los abuelos. Me gustaba mucho porque había muchos regalos. Siempre jugaba con mis primos.*

**E.** Read your paragraph and check for correct spelling and vocabulary use. Share your paragraph with a partner, who should check the following:

_____ Is the paragraph easy to understand?

_____ Is there anything you should add?

_____ Are there any errors?

## A ver si recuerdas: Expressions using *tener* (p. 237)

• Remember that **tener** is used in many expressions when English uses "to be."

| | |
|---|---|
| **Marta tiene prisa.** *Marta is in a hurry.* | **Tengo hambre.** *I am hungry.* |
| **Luisito tiene ocho años.** *Luisito is eight years old.* | **Tengo sed.** *I am thirsty.* |
| **Tenemos razón.** *We are right.* | **Tienes cuidado.** *You are careful.* |
| **Ellos tienen miedo.** *They are afraid.* | **Tengo calor.** *I am warm/hot.* |
| **Los estudiantes tienen sueño.** *The students are tired.* | **Tengo frío.** *I am cold.* |

**A.** Read each statement and choose the appropriate phrase within the parentheses. Follow the model.

> **Modelo**   Necesito beber algo. Yo ( **tengo hambre** / (**tengo sed**) ).

1. Juana quiere dormir ahora. Ella ( **tiene sueño** / **tiene prisa** ).

2. Nosotros sabemos mucho. Creemos que ( **tenemos razón** / **tenemos miedo** ).

3. Los niños miran en todas las direcciones antes de cruzar la calle. Ellos
   ( **tienen frío** / **tienen cuidado** ).

4. La temperatura está a ochenta y cinco grados. Tú ( **tienes razón** / **tienes calor** ).

5. Yo veo un oso en las montañas. Yo ( **tengo miedo** / **tengo hambre** ).

**B.** Write the correct **tener** expression according to each picture. Remember to conjugate **tener**. Follow the model.

> **Modelo**   Ellos ____*tienen*____ ____*hambre*____.

1. Jorge _____ _____.

2. Yo _____ _____.

3. ¡Nosotros _____ _____!

4. Tú _____ _____.

# A ver si recuerdas: The use of *¡Qué...!* in exclamations (p. 237)

• As you know, **¡Qué...!** is used with adverbs and adjectives to exclaim "How . . . !"

| | |
|---|---|
| **¡Qué buenos son mis estudiantes!** | *How good my students are!* |
| **¡Qué pronto llegaron!** | *How quickly they arrived!* |

**A.** Read the following statements and circle the appropriate reaction. The first one is done for you.

1. El gato de Juan está enfermo. ( **¡Qué triste!** / **¡Qué feo!** )

2. Llegamos a Boston en sólo cuarenta y cinco minutos. ( **¡Qué rápido!** / **¡Qué sabroso!** )

3. Mmmmm. Me encantan las galletas de mi mamá. ( **¡Qué graciosas!** / **¡Qué sabrosas!** )

4. Me gustan las flores de tu jardín. ( **¡Qué lentas!** / **¡Qué bonitas!** )

5. Mi hijo saca buenas notas en todas sus clases. ( **¡Qué inteligente!** / **¡Qué guapo!** )

• As you know **¡Qué ...!** is used with nouns to say "What (a) . . . !"

| | |
|---|---|
| **¡Qué bailarina es tu novia!** | *What a dancer your girlfriend is!* |

**B.** Read the statements below and complete the exclamations with the appropriate nouns. Follow the model.

**Modelo**   Tu hijo es un estudiante muy bueno.   ¡Qué _____*estudiante*_____ es tu hijo!

1. María es una cocinera fantástica.   ¡Qué _____ es María!

2. Los hermanos Rulfo son increíbles jugadores de fútbol.   ¡Qué _____ son los hermanos Rulfo!

3. Yo soy un buen músico.   ¡Qué _____ soy yo!

4. Nosotros somos doctores fantásticos.   ¡Qué _____ somos nosotros!

Write the Spanish vocabulary word below each picture. Be sure to include the article for each noun.

Write the Spanish vocabulary word below each picture. Be sure to include the article for each noun.

_____

_____

_____

_____

_____

_____

_____

_____

_____

_____

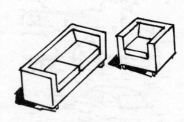

_____

_____

_____

_____

_____

_____

_____

_____

Write the Spanish vocabulary word below each picture. Be sure to include the article for each noun.

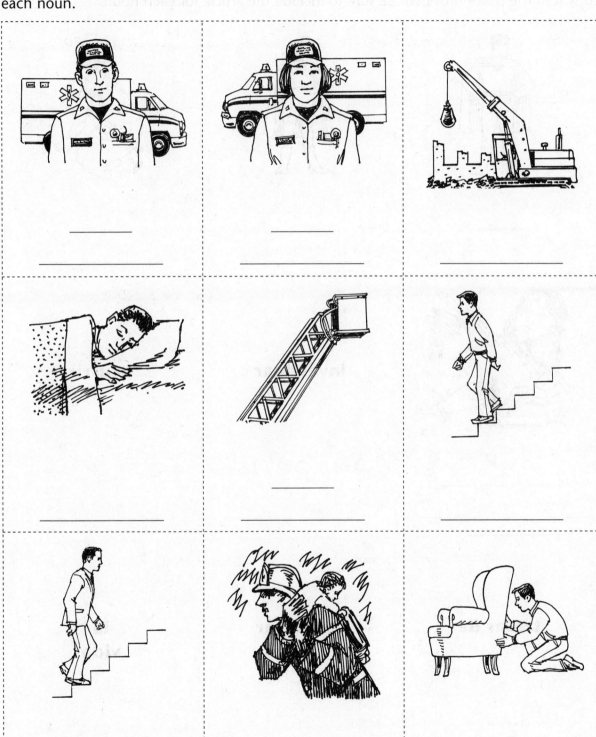

Nombre _____    Hora _____

**Capítulo 5A**    Fecha _____    **Vocabulary Flash Cards, Sheet 4**

Write the Spanish vocabulary word below each picture. If there is a word or phrase, copy it in the space provided. Be sure to include the article for each noun.

investigar

ocurrir

tratar de

comenzar

la
vida

**166**  *Guided Practice Activities* — *Vocabulary Flash Cards 5A*

**Capítulo 5A**

Copy the word or phrase in the space provided. Be sure to include the article for each noun.

| | | |
|---|---|---|
| **escaparse** | **muerto, muerta** | **herido, herida** |
| _____ | _____ , _____ | _____ , _____ |
| **el herido, la herida** | **salvar** | **valiente** |
| _____ _____ , _____ | _____ | _____ |
| **vivo, viva** | **a causa de** | **asustado, asustada** |
| _____ , _____ | _____ _____ _____ | _____ , _____ |

Copy the word or phrase in the space provided. Be sure to include the article for each noun.

| | | |
|---|---|---|
| **la causa** | **de prisa** | **de repente** |
| _____ | _____ | _____ |
| _____ | _____ | _____ |
| **gritar** | **hubo** | **se murieron** |
| | | _____ |
| _____ | _____ | _____ |
| **oír** | **sin duda** | **el noticiero** |
| | _____ | _____ |
| _____ | _____ | _____ |

Copy the word or phrase in the space provided. Be sure to include the article for each noun. The blank cards can be used to write and practice other Spanish vocabulary for the chapter.

| | | |
|---|---|---|
| **afortunadamente** | **la tormenta** | **quemar(se)** |
| _____ | _____ | _____ |
| | | |
| _____ | _____ | _____ |
| | | |
| _____ | _____ | _____ |

These blank cards can be used to write and practice other Spanish vocabulary for the chapter.

_____      _____      _____

_____      _____      _____

_____      _____      _____

Tear out this page. Write the English words on the lines. Fold the paper along the dotted line to see the correct answers so you can check your work.

llover                          _____

nevar                          _____

el terremoto                   _____

la tormenta                    _____

el artículo                    _____

el locutor,                    _____
la locutora

el noticiero                   _____

ocurrir                        _____

el reportero,                  _____
la reportera

apagar                         _____

el bombero,                    _____
la bombera

la escalera                    _____

escaparse                      _____

esconderse                     _____

Fold In
→

**Capítulo 5A**

Fecha _____ **Vocabulary Check, Sheet 2**

Tear out this page. Write the Spanish words on the lines. Fold the paper along the dotted line to see the correct answers so you can check your work.

to rain _____

to snow _____

earthquake _____

storm _____

article _____

announcer _____

newscast _____

to occur _____

reporter _____

to put out (fire) _____

firefighter _____

ladder _____

to escape _____

to hide (oneself) _____

Fold In

Tear out this page. Write the English words on the lines. Fold the paper along the
dotted line to see the correct answers so you can check your work.

el humo _____

el incendio _____

el paramédico,
la paramédica _____

quemar(se) _____


el herido, la herida _____

rescatar _____

salvar _____

la vida _____

vivo, viva _____

afortunadamente _____

asustado, asustada _____

la causa _____

gritar _____

¡Socorro! _____

Fold In

Tear out this page. Write the Spanish words on the lines. Fold the paper along the dotted line to see the correct answers so you can check your work.

smoke _____

fire _____

paramedic _____

to burn (oneself),
to burn up _____

injured person _____

to rescue _____

to save _____

life _____

living, alive _____

fortunately _____

frightened _____

cause _____

to scream _____

Help! _____

Fold In

**Capítulo 5A**

# The imperfect tense: other uses (p. 248)

- You can use the imperfect tense to tell what time it was (**qué hora era**), or what the weather was like (**qué tiempo hacía**) when something happened.

  *Eran* **las cinco de la mañana cuando el huracán comenzó.**

  *It was five in the morning when the hurricane began.*

**A.** Read the following statements and circle the verb that tells what time it was or what the weather was like (the imperfect tense). Then, underline the verb that gives the action (the preterite tense).

Modelo ( (Eran) / Fueron ) las diez de la noche cuando <u>terminó</u> el noticiero.

1. ( Llovía / Llovió ) mucho cuando me levanté.

2. ( Nevó / Nevaba ) cuando salí de casa.

3. ( Eran / Fueron ) las tres de la tarde cuando comenzó el huracán.

4. ( Hubo / Había ) una tormenta de lluvia cuando comenzó la inundación.

5. ( Era / Eran ) la una de la tarde cuando vi el incendio.

6. ( Eran / Era ) las nueve cuando me acosté.

7. ( Hacía / Hacían ) mal tiempo cuando llegué a casa.

**B.** Write the imperfect form of the verb in parentheses to complete the weather description or time expression in each sentence below. Follow the model.

Modelo (**Ser**) _____*Eran*_____ las cuatro cuando la explosión ocurrió.

1. (**Hacer**) _____ mucho viento cuando los paramédicos llegaron.

2. Cuando la locutora comenzó a hablar, (**ser**) _____ las seis de la noche.

3. Cuando chocaron esos tres coches, (**hacer**) _____ mal tiempo.

4. (**Llover**) _____ mucho cuando ocurrió el accidente.

5. (**Ser**) _____ las doce cuando mi hermano volvió a casa.

**Capítulo 5A**

Fecha _____

# The imperfect tense: other uses (*continued*)

- The imperfect tense is also used to tell how a person was feeling when something happened.

  **Anoche me acosté temprano porque *tenía* sueño.**

  *Last night I went to bed early because I was sleepy.*

**C.** In each sentence, underline the preterite verb, which tells what action took place. Then, complete the sentence with the imperfect form of the verb in parentheses to tell how the people were feeling. The first one is done for you.

1. <u>Fuimos</u> a comer algo porque nosotros _____*teníamos*_____ hambre. (**tener**)

2. La reportera habló con muchas personas porque ella _____ (**querer**) saber qué ocurrió.

3. Los paramédicos _____ (**tener**) prisa, y por eso salieron pronto.

4. Cuando apagaron el incendio, los bomberos _____ (**querer**) descansar.

5. Cuando llegamos al edificio, nosotros _____ (**estar**) nerviosos.

6. Juanita gritó porque ella _____ (**estar**) asustada.

**D.** You have learned three ways to tell about events in the past using the imperfect and preterite tenses in this chapter. Use the graphic below to create three sentences in the past. Remember to conjugate the verbs! Follow the model.

**Modelo**

| Telling Time | cuando | Action |
| Ser las siete de la tarde | | nosotros ver el noticiero |

*Eran las siete de la tarde cuando nosotros vimos el noticiero.*

1.

| How they feel | porque | Action |
| Los paramédicos estar cansados | | subir las escaleras de prisa |

_____

2.

| The weather | cuando | Action |
| Hacer mucho viento | | el huracán llegar a la ciudad |

_____

3.

| Telling time | cuando | Action |
| Ser las cinco y media de la tarde | | los bomberos apagar el incendio |

_____

# The imperfect tense: other uses *(continued)*

- Remember that **hubo** and **había** are forms of **haber**. Both words mean "there was" or "there were." Look at these rules:
- Use **hubo** to say that an event (such as a fire) took place.
  **Hubo un incendio ayer.**   *There was a fire. = it took place*
- Use **había** to describe a situation in the past.
  **Había mucho humo en el edificio.**   *There was smoke in the building. = the condition existed*

**E.** Below there are two sentences in the past for each drawing: one tells about an action and the other gives a description. If the sentence tells that an action took place, write **hubo**. If the sentence describes a situation or condition that existed, write **había**. Follow the models.

**Modelos**

_____*Hubo*_____ una tormenta muy mala.

_____*Había*_____ muchos árboles en la calle.

1. _____ un terremoto en esta ciudad.

2. _____ poca gente en las calles.

3. _____ muchos heridos.

4. _____ un incendio a las siete de la mañana.

5. _____ una inundación en la ciudad.

6. _____ muchas casas destruidas.

# The preterite of the verbs *oír, creer, leer,* and *destruir* (p. 250)

- The verbs **oír, creer, leer,** and **destruir** are irregular in the preterite.
- These verbs are irregular in the **Ud./él/ella** and **Uds./ellos/ellas** forms. Instead of an "i" on the endings there is a "y".
- The verbs **oír, leer,** and **creer** have accent marks on the **tú, nosotros/nosotras** and **vosotros/vosotras** forms, whereas **destruir** does not.

| yo | oí | leí | creí | destruí |
|---|---|---|---|---|
| tú | oíste | leíste | creíste | destruiste |
| usted/él/ella | oyó | leyó | creyó | destruyó |
| nosotros/nosotras | oímos | leímos | creímos | destruimos |
| vosotros/vosotras | oísteis | leísteis | creísteis | destruisteis |
| ustedes/ellos/ellas | oyeron | leyeron | creyeron | destruyeron |

**A.** Read the sentences below and look at the underlined verbs. Write an **X** in either the **Present** or the **Preterite** column, according to the tense of the underlined verb. The first one is done for you.

|  | Present | Preterite |
|---|---|---|
| 1. Anoche <u>oí</u> un grito en la casa. | _____ | __X__ |
| 2. Ella <u>oye</u> al locutor por la radio. | _____ | _____ |
| 3. ¿Tú <u>crees</u> que la gente se escapó? | _____ | _____ |
| 4. Nosotros <u>creímos</u> al reportero. | _____ | _____ |
| 5. El incendio <u>destruyó</u> el edificio de apartamentos. | _____ | _____ |
| 6. Anoche Amalia <u>leyó</u> el artículo del terremoto. | _____ | _____ |

**B.** Complete the following sentences with the correct form of the verb in parentheses.

1. Ayer tú _____ (**oír**) el noticiero en la radio.
2. Mis padres _____ (**creer**) las noticias.
3. El huracán _____ (**destruir**) las casas.
4. Los bomberos _____ (**oír**) la explosión.
5. El incendio _____ (**destruir**) los muebles.
6. Los estudiantes _____ (**leer**) las noticias en la biblioteca.

Nombre _____ Hora _____

**Capítulo 5A**

Fecha _____

Guided Practice Activities **5A-5**

## Lectura: Desastre en Valdivia, Chile (pp. 256–257)

**A.** The reading in your textbook is about natural disasters that occurred in Valdivia, Chile. Think of four things that you already know about earthquakes and tsunamis, and write them below.

1. _____     3. _____

2. _____     4. _____

**B.** Cognates are words that are similar in spelling and pronunciation. Here are some sentences from your textbook reading, in which some of the Spanish words have been circled. Write the English cognates beneath each set of sentences.

1. A las seis y dos (minutos) de la mañana, el 21 de (mayo) 1960, una gran (parte) del país sintió el primer terremoto.

   a. _____     b. _____     c. _____

2. Unos minutos después del (desastroso) terremoto, llegó un (tsunami) que destruyó lo poco que quedaba en la ciudad y en las pequeñas (comunidades.)

   a. _____     b. _____     c. _____

3. La gran ola de agua se levantó (destruyendo) a su paso casas, (animales,) botes y, por supuesto, muchas vidas (humanas.)

   a. _____     b. _____     c. _____

**C.** Read the following rules from your textbook reading about what to do and what not to do during an earthquake. Place an **X** next to the things you should do in the **Sí** column, and should not do in the **No** column.

**Si estás en un edificio durante un terremoto:**               Sí          No

1. Debes mantener la calma.                                 _____     _____

2. Debes mantenerte cerca de las ventanas.                 _____     _____

3. Debes utilizar los elevadores.                          _____     _____

**Si estás fuera de un edificio durante un terremoto:**

4. Debes estar lejos de los postes de energía eléctrica.   _____     _____

5. Debes ir a un edificio alto.                            _____     _____

**Capítulo 5A**

# Presentación oral (p. 259)

**Task:** You and a partner will role-play an interview about an imaginary fire that happened in your town or city. You will need to create a list of questions and answers for the interview. Use your lists during the interview.

**A.** Read the following phrases. Write **dónde** if the phrase describes *where* the fire happened. Write **cuándo** if it describes *when* it happened. Write **quién** if it names people *who* were involved. Write **por qué** if it describes *why* it happened. Follow the model.

**Modelo**    problema eléctrico ____*por qué*____

1. en una escuela    _____
2. ayer por la noche    _____
3. una explosión    _____
4. muchos niños    _____

5. a las cinco de la mañana    _____
6. un cable eléctrico    _____
7. en un edificio    _____
8. algunas personas    _____

**B.** Use the information from **part A** or make up your own to answer the following questions about the fire. The first one is done for you.

1. ¿Dónde fue el incendio? *El incendio fue en un edificio.* _____

2. ¿Cuándo ocurrió? _____

3. ¿Quiénes estaban allí? _____

4. ¿Por qué ocurrió? _____

**C.** Use the questions and your answers from **part B** to practice for the interview.

**D.** Your teacher will tell you which role to play. Listen to your partner's questions or answers and keep the interview going. Remember that you should ask or tell "when," "where," and "why" the imaginary fire occurred, and "who" was involved. Complete the paragraph below to start the interview.

Anoche hubo un incendio en _____. Los bomberos estuvieron

allí _____. _____ se salvaron.

El incendio ocurrió porque _____

Write the Spanish vocabulary word or phrase below each picture. Be sure to include the article for each noun.

_____ _____

_____ _____

_____ _____

_____ _____

_____ _____

_____ _____

_____ _____

_____ _____

_____

_____

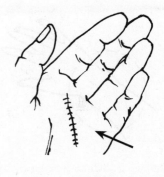

_____ _____

_____ _____

_____

_____

_____

_____

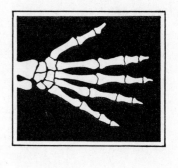

_____ _____

_____ _____

Write the Spanish vocabulary word below each picture. Be sure to include the article for each noun.

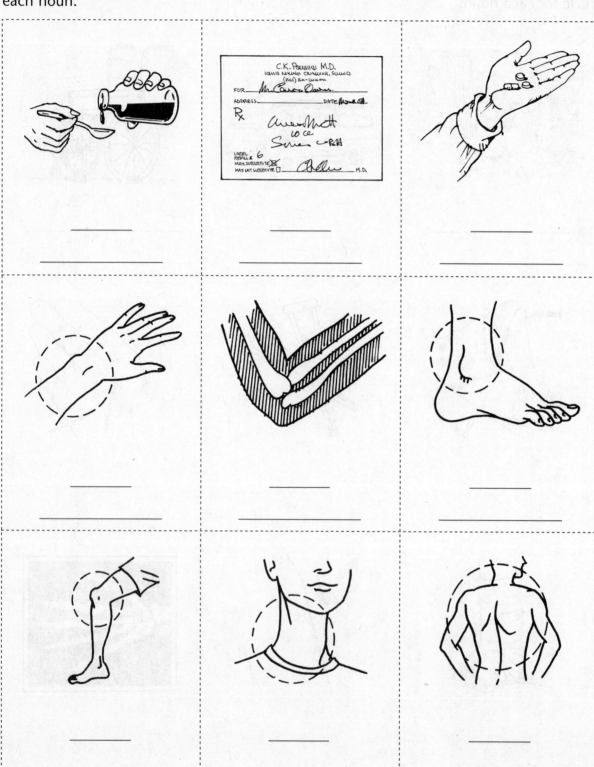

**Capítulo 5B**   Fecha _____   **Vocabulary Flash Cards, Sheet 3**

Write the Spanish vocabulary word or phrase below each picture. Be sure to include the article for each noun.

**Capítulo 5B**   Fecha _____   **Vocabulary Flash Cards, Sheet 4**

Write the Spanish vocabulary word below each picture. If there is a word or phrase, copy it in the space provided. Be sure to include the article for each noun.

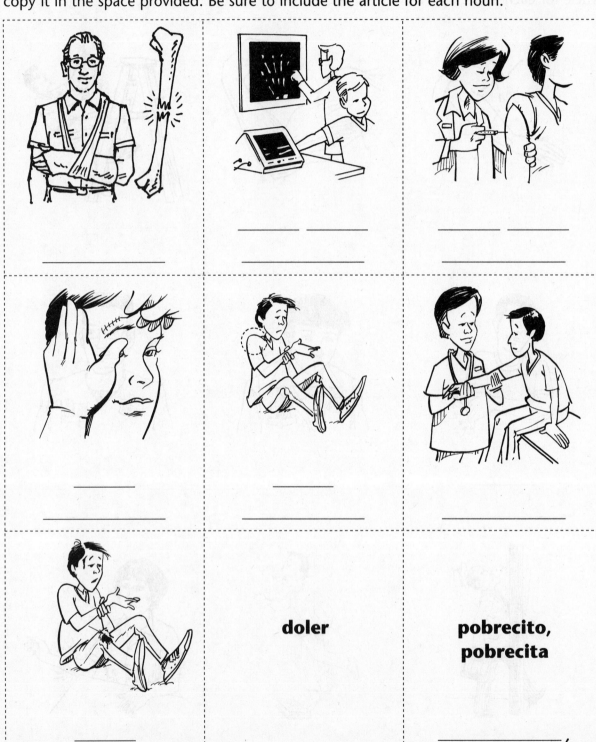

doler

pobrecito, pobrecita

Copy the word or phrase in the space provided. Be sure to include the article for each noun.

| | | |
|---|---|---|
| **la sangre** <br><br><br> _____ <br> _____ | **recetar** <br><br><br><br> _____ | **roto, rota** <br><br><br> _____ , <br> _____ |
| **me caigo** <br><br><br> _____ <br> _____ | **el accidente** <br><br><br> _____ <br> _____ | **te caes** <br><br><br> _____ <br> _____ |
| **se cayeron** <br><br><br> _____ <br> _____ | **cortarse** <br><br><br><br> _____ | **¿Qué te pasó?** <br><br><br> _____ _____ <br> _____ |

Copy the word or phrase in the space provided. The blank cards can be used to write and practice other Spanish vocabulary for the chapter.

| | | |
|---|---|---|
| **torcerse** | **sentirse** | **moverse** |
| _____ | _____ | _____ |
| **¡Qué lástima!** | | |
| _____ | _____ | _____ |
| | | |
| _____ | _____ | _____ |

Tear out this page. Write the English words on the lines. Fold the paper along the dotted line to see the correct answers so you can check your work.

el enfermero,
la enfermera        _____

la inyección        _____

la medicina         _____

las pastillas       _____

las puntadas        _____

la radiografía      _____

la receta           _____

la sala de
emergencia          _____

la sangre           _____

la venda            _____

el yeso             _____

el accidente        _____

la ambulancia       _____

cortarse            _____

lastimarse          _____

Fold In ←

Tear out this page. Write the Spanish words on the lines. Fold the paper along the dotted line to see the correct answers so you can check your work.

nurse _____

injection, shot _____

medicine _____

pills _____

stitches _____

X-ray _____

prescription _____

emergency room _____

blood _____

bandage _____

cast _____

accident _____

ambulance _____

to cut oneself _____

to hurt oneself _____

Fold In

Tear out this page. Write the English words on the lines. Fold the paper along the
dotted line to see the correct answers so you can check your work.

romperse          _____

torcerse          _____

tropezar (con)    _____

el codo           _____

el cuello         _____

la espalda        _____

el hombro         _____

el hueso          _____

la muñeca         _____

el músculo        _____

la rodilla        _____

el tobillo        _____

pobrecito,        _____
pobrecita

Fold In

Nombre _____   Hora _____

**Capítulo 5B**   Fecha _____   **Vocabulary Check, Sheet 4**

Tear out this page. Write the Spanish words on the lines. Fold the paper along the dotted line to see the correct answers so you can check your work.

to break, to tear _____

to twist, to sprain _____

to trip (over) _____

elbow _____

neck _____

back _____

shoulder _____

bone _____

wrist _____

muscle _____

knee _____

ankle _____

poor thing _____

Fold In

# Irregular preterites: *venir, poner, decir,* and *traer* (p. 274)

- The verbs **venir, poner, decir,** and **traer** have a similar pattern in the preterite as that of **estar, poder,** and **tener.** They have irregular stems. Remember that the endings do not have any accent marks.

| Infinitive | Stem |
|------------|-------|
| decir | dij- |
| estar | estuv- |
| poder | pud- |
| poner | pus- |
| tener | tuv- |
| traer | traj- |
| venir | vin- |

| Irregular Preterite Endings | |
|------|------|
| -e | -imos |
| -iste | -isteis |
| -o | -ieron, -eron |

| Preterite of *venir* | |
|------|------|
| vine | vinimos |
| viniste | vinisteis |
| vino | vinieron |

**A.** Look at the drawings showing what happened to Diego. Then, read the paragraph and circle the correct irregular preterite form of the verb in parentheses. The first one has been done for you.

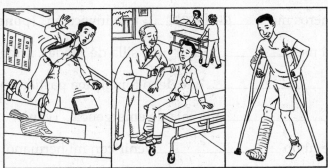

Ayer Diego ( **tuve** / **tuvo** ) un accidente. Sus padres ( **vino** / **vinieron** ) a la escuela

porque Diego ( **tuvo** / **tuve** ) que ir a la sala de emergencia. Yo fui con ellos.

Nosotros ( **estuvieron** / **estuvimos** ) con él en el hospital por seis horas. Diego no

( **pudo** / **pudiste** ) moverse por dos horas. Después, el enfermero le

( **trajo** / **trajimos** ) una venda y le ( **puso** / **pusieron** ) la venda en el brazo.

El enfermero ( **dije** / **dijo** ) que su brazo no estaba roto pero ellos le

( **pusimos** / **pusieron** ) un yeso en el tobillo. Luego, Diego ( **tuvo** / **tuvieron** ) que

caminar con muletas. Yo le ( **dijiste** / **dije** ) a Diego que quería escribir mi nombre

en el yeso.

## Irregular preterites: *venir, poner, decir,* and *traer* (*continued*)

**B.** Look at the sentences below and fill in the missing stem of the verb in parentheses for each ending that is given. Follow the model.

> **Modelo**   (traer) La enfermera me _____*traj*_o una silla de ruedas.

1. (**venir**) Todos _____ieron a la sala de emergencia conmigo.

2. (**decir**) Tú _____iste "¡Ay!" cuando te lastimaste.

3. (**traer**) Nosotros le _____imos una venda y medicina.

4. (**poner**) La enfermera me _____o una inyección.

5. (**estar**) La familia _____o en el hospital por cuatro horas.

6. (**tener**) El coche _____o un accidente anoche.

7. (**poder**) Yo no _____e ver lo que pasó.

**C.** The following actions happened in the past. Write in the correct form of the verb in parentheses to complete each sentence. Follow the model.

> **Modelo**   Los enfermeros me _____*pusieron*_____ una inyección.  (**poner**)

1. Mi mamá y papá me _____ una silla de ruedas.  (**traer**)

2. El enfermero me _____ que debo tomar una pastilla para el dolor.  (**decir**)

3. Mi hermano _____ a la sala de emergencia.  (**venir**)

4. ¡Qué lástima que tú no _____ venir con mi hermano!  (**poder**)

5. Yo no _____ en la sala de emergencia anoche.  (**estar**)

6. Nosotros _____ que salir del edificio porque un incendio comenzó.
   (**tener**)

7. Por desgracia, nadie _____ botellas de agua.  (**traer**)

# Imperfect progressive and preterite (p. 277)

- Remember that the present progressive is used to tell what someone is doing. It is formed by the present tense of the verb **estar** + present participle (-**ando** or -**iendo**):

  **La doctora está hablando.**            *The doctor is talking.*

  **Laura y Juan están corriendo.**        *Laura and Juan are running.*

- As shown above, the present progressive is used to tell what *is* happening. The imperfect progressive is used to tell what *was* happening. It uses the imperfect tense of **estar** + present participle:

  **La doctora estaba hablando.**          *The doctor was talking.*

  **Laura y Juan estaban corriendo.**      *Laura and Juan were running.*

**A.** First, circle the present progressive in each sentence. Then, change each sentence from the present progressive to the *imperfect* progressive. Follow the model.

| Modelo | Eliana (está caminando) con muletas. | *estaba* | *caminando* |

1. Juana está hablando con el doctor.            _____ _____

2. Nosotros estamos bebiendo bastante agua.      _____ _____

3. Yo estoy examinando las puntadas.             _____ _____

4. Tú estás sacando una radiografía.             _____ _____

5. La enfermera está poniendo una inyección.     _____ _____

6. El doctor me está dando puntadas.             _____ _____

7. Los paramédicos le están moviendo a otro piso. _____ _____

- You can use the imperfect progressive tense to describe something that was happening over a period of time. The imperfect progressive uses the imperfect tense of **estar** + the present participle:

  **Teresa estaba escribiendo un cuento.**        *Teresa was writing a story.*

**B.** The following sentences tell what people were doing yesterday in the hospital when the storm began. Complete each sentence by writing in the correct form of **estar** and the participle of the verb in parentheses. Follow the model.

**Cuando la tormenta comenzó…**

| Modelo | Mario _____*estaba*_____ _____*caminando*_____ con muletas. (**caminar**) |

1. mi hermano _____ _____ una radiografía. (**sacar**)

2. mis amigos y yo _____ _____ la ambulancia. (**esperar**)

# Imperfect progressive and preterite (*continued*)

3. la Dra. Carrillo _____ _____ una receta. (**escribir**)

4. usted _____ _____ a Javier. (**ayudar**)

5. tú _____ _____ una inyección. (**poner**)

- Remember that some present participles have changes in their spelling.
- **-ir** stem-changing verbs have a vowel change to "i" or "u":

  pedir → **pidiendo**    vestir → **vistiendo**    dormir → **durmiendo**

- **leer, caer, creer,** and **traer** have a "y":

  leer → **leyendo**    caer → **cayendo**    creer → **creyendo**    traer → **trayendo**

**C.** A paramedic has to report to his boss about what different patients were doing when they got hurt. Complete his statements. Follow the model.

Modelo   Los niños / seguir / a sus hermanos mayores

*Los niños estaban siguiendo a sus hermanos mayores* .

1. Los camareros / servir / sopa muy caliente

_____ .

2. Felipe Sánchez / leer / una novela muy interesante

_____ .

3  Adelita Romero / vestir / a su perro

_____ .

4. Nosotros / subir / las escaleras

_____ .

5. El señor Peña / dormir / en el sofá

_____ .

# Imperfect progressive and preterite (*continued*)

- The imperfect progressive and the preterite tenses can be used in the same sentence. The imperfect progressive describes what was happening while the preterite tells about something specific that happened or that interrupted an action.

    **Ella estaba corriendo cuando se lastimó el tobillo.**
    *She was running when she hurt her ankle.*

**D.** For each sentence below, draw a line beneath the verb in the imperfect progressive tense that identifies what was happening. Then, identify the interrupted action by circling the verb in the preterite tense. The first one is done for you.

1. Yo <u>estaba corriendo</u> cuando (tropecé.)

2. Cuando Miguel se lastimó, él estaba jugando al fútbol.

3. Tú estabas sirviendo la comida cuando te lastimaste.

4. Las hermanas Paulatino estaban usando la silla de ruedas cuando tuvieron el accidente.

5. Cuando Teresa llegó a la sala de emergencia le estaba doliendo mucho el brazo.

**E.** The sentences below describe what different people were doing when something bad happened to them. Read the sentences and circle the verb that completes each sentence in the most logical way. Follow the model.

**Modelo**    Antonio ( (estaba jugando) / jugó ) al tenis cuando se lastimó la rodilla.

1. María y Fernando estaban esquiando cuando ( se estaban cayendo / se cayeron ).

2. Nosotros estábamos peleándonos cuando yo ( me estaba rompiendo / me rompí ) el dedo.

3. MaríaTeresa ( estaba caminando / caminó ) a casa sin chaqueta cuando comenzó a nevar.

4. Cuando yo me lastimé, ( estaba corriendo / corrí ) un maratón.

**F.** Look at the information in the boxes below. Use the imperfect progressive and the preterite to fill in the blanks with the phrases contained in the boxes. Follow the model.

**Modelo**

| What was happening | Specific occurrence that took place |
|---|---|
| levantar pesas | lastimarse |

Marcos ___*estaba levantando pesas*___ cuando ___*se lastimó*___ el hombro.

1.

| What was happening | Specific occurrence that took place |
|---|---|
| usar tijeras | cortarse |

Tú _____ cuando _____ el dedo.

# Imperfect progressive and preterite (*continued*)

2.

| What was happening | Specific occurrence that took place |
|---|---|
| leer el periódico | ver |

Maricarmen _____ cuando _____ del accidente.

3.

| What was happening | Specific occurrence that took place |
|---|---|
| pedir una silla de ruedas | caerse |

Yo _____ cuando _____ .

4.

| What was happening | Specific occurrence that took place |
|---|---|
| vestirse | sentir dolor |

Tú _____ cuando _____ en la espalda.

- When you use pronouns with the imperfect progressive, you can put them before **estar** or attach them to the participle. Remember to add an accent over the "e" or "a" of the participle ending.

    **Yo me estaba sirviendo.** *or:* **Yo estaba sirviéndome.**

**G.** Rewrite the sentences below by putting the underlined object pronoun after the conjugated present partciple. Follow the model.

**Modelo** Javier se estaba cepillando los dientes.

_Javier estaba cepillándose los dientes_____ .

1. Tía Luisa me estaba trayendo un sándwich.

   _____

2. Cristina y Julia nos estaban pidiendo ayuda.

   _____

3. Tú te estabas duchando.

   _____

4. Nosotros nos estábamos levantando.

   _____

**Capítulo 5B**

Fecha _____

## Lectura: Mejorar la salud para todos (pp. 282–283)

**A.** The articles in your textbook reading are about health organizations. A good strategy for understanding these articles is to look for cognates. The following words are cognates from the reading. Say each word in Spanish aloud and then write the letter of the English word that matches it.

1. _____ internacional     **a.** international     **b.** internal

2. _____ institución     **a.** institution     **b.** inspiration

3. _____ promover     **a.** protect     **b.** promote

4. _____ prolongar     **a.** prolong     **b.** protect

5. _____ voluntarios     **a.** volume     **b.** volunteers

**B.** Look at this title from one of the health articles in your textbook. Then, read the sentences that follow and write **L** (for **Lectura**) if it's something you read in the title. Write **N** (for **No**) if it's something you didn't read in the title.

> *Cuerpo de la Paz* (Peace Corps) *y Medical Aid for Children of Latin America* (MACLA) *ayudan a niños que requieren cirugía plástica* (plastic surgery).

1. MACLA significa *Medical Aid for Children of Latin America.* _____

2. Cuerpo de la Paz y MACLA ayudan a niños que requieren cirugía plástica. _____

3. Los niños son de Europa. _____

**C.** The following are quotes from the reading in your textbook. Read what was said by the singers José Luis Carreras and Jennifer López. Then, circle the option that best completes each sentence.

> *"No podéis imaginar lo que significa para nosotros, los enfermos, disponer de un donante de sangre o de células madre. Es un acto de solidaridad y de altruismo, algo que seguro os hará sentir orgullosos de vosotros mismos."* –José Luis Carreras
>
> *"Quiero ayudar a la gente. Es el mismo tipo de sueño que tenía con el baile, y que me está llevando a hacer algo bueno por el mundo."* –Jennifer López

1. José Luis Carreras speaks about
   **a.** donating blood or bone marrow.
   **b.** vaccinations.

2. Jennifer López speaks about
   **a.** the prevention of drug abuse.
   **b.** helping people.

## Capítulo 5B

Fecha _____

# Presentación escrita (p. 285)

**Task:** Imagine you have to report an accident you saw near school. Organize your ideas before you write the report for your school.

**A.** First, you need to describe what you were doing when the accident occurred. Choose an activity from the list below. Then, circle the activity.

### ¿Qué estabas haciendo?

**1.** Estaba saliendo de la escuela.

**4.** Estaba entrando en la escuela.

**2.** Estaba jugando con mis amigos.

**5.** Estaba caminando con mi hermano.

**3.** Estaba hablando con la profesora.

**B.** Next, the chart below can help you organize information about the accident. You need to determine: What happened? When did it happen? Who was hurt? Who helped? Circle one option in each column.

| ¿Qué pasó? | ¿Cuándo ocurrió? | ¿Quién se lastimó? | ¿Quiénes ayudaron? |
|---|---|---|---|
| un árbol se cayó | por la mañana | un estudiante <br> una estudiante | los estudiantes |
| un coche chocó con algo | por la tarde | un profesor <br> una profesora | los bomberos |
| una ventana se rompió | por la noche | una señora <br> un hombre | una enfermera <br> la policía |

**C.** Now, use your answers from **parts A** and **B** to complete a report of the accident. You can follow the model below.

Yo _____ cuando vi un accidente. _____

_____ y _____ se lastimó.

_____ lo/la ayudó.

**D.** Read through your accident report to check for spelling, correct verb usage, vocabulary, and clarity.

**E.** Share the report with a partner who should check the following:

_____ Is the report easy to understand?

_____ Is the information in a clear, logical order?

_____ Is there anything to add to give more information?

_____ Are there any errors?

# A ver si recuerdas: Verbs like *gustar* (p. 291)

- You are already familiar with the verb **gustar** and other verbs that function like it (**encantar, disgustar, importar, interesar**). Remember that the verb agrees in number with the item or action that follows it. The indirect object pronoun agrees with the person whose preferences are geing discussed.

      **A Juan → le encantan los deportes.**
      *Juan loves sports.*

      **A nosotros → nos importa el partido de tenis.**
      *The tennis match is important to us.*

**A.** Write the indirect object pronoun that corresponds to the person listed below. The indirect object pronouns are in the box below to help you.

| **me** | *to me* | **nos** | *to us* |
|--------|---------|---------|---------|
| **te** | *to you (sing.)* | **os** | *to you (pl.)* |
| **le** | *to him/her* <br> *to you (form.)* | **les** | *to them* <br> *to you (pl.)* |

**Modelo**   Al profesor Rodríguez ____*le*____

1. A Juliana _____

2. A nosotros _____

3. A mí _____

4. A los doctores _____

5. A ti _____

6. A Juan y a Ramón _____

7. A ustedes _____

8. A mi hermano y a mí _____

9. A la profesora _____

10. A usted _____

# Verbs like *gustar* (*continued*)

**B.** Look at the picture and corresponding noun for each number. Circle the correct form of the verb that could be used in a sentence about the noun.

Modelo  ( encanta / (encantan) ) las películas de horror

1. ( **disgusta** / **disgustan** ) las telenovelas

2. ( **gusta** / **gustan** ) el cine

3. ( **interesa** / **interesan** ) los programas deportivos

4. ( **importa** / **importan** ) la televisión

5. ( **encanta** / **encantan** ) los programas musicales

**C.** Now complete these sentences, which are combined from exercises A and B. Write the appropriate indirect object pronoun in the first blank, and the correct form of the verb given in the second blank. Follow the model.

Modelo   A mí ___me___ ___encantan___ (encantar) los programas musicales.

1. A Juan y a Ramón _____ _____ (**interesar**) los programas deportivos.

2. A mi hermano y a mí _____ _____ (**importar**) la televisión.

3. A Juliana _____ _____ (**gustar**) el cine.

4. A nosotros _____ _____ (**encantar**) las películas de horror.

5. A ustedes _____ _____ (**disgustar**) las telenovelas.

6. A ti _____ _____ (**encantar**) los programas musicales.

Nombre _____ Hora _____

Fecha _____ **Vocabulary Flash Cards, Sheet 1**

Write the Spanish vocabulary word below each picture. Be sure to include the article for each noun.

_____

_____

_____

_____

_____

_____

_____

_____

_____

_____

_____

_____

_____

_____

_____

_____

_____

_____

Write the Spanish vocabulary word below each picture. Be sure to include the article for each noun.

_____

_____

_____

_____

_____

_____

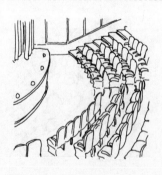

_____

_____

_____

**Capítulo 6A** | Fecha _____ | **Vocabulary Flash Cards, Sheet 3**

Write the Spanish vocabulary word or phrase below each picture. Be sure to include the article for each noun.

_____
_____

_____
_____

_____
_____

_____
_____

_____
_____

_____
_____

_____
_____

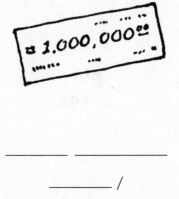

_____ /
_____

_____
_____

Copy the word or phrase in the space provided. Be sure to include the article for each noun.

| | | |
|---|---|---|
| **enojado, enojada** | **furioso, furiosa** | **agitado, agitada** |
| _____ , _____ | _____ , _____ | _____ , _____ |
| **al final** | **la competencia** | **fenomenal** |
| _____ _____ | _____ _____ | _____ |
| **la liga** | **por ... vez** | **resultar** |
| _____ _____ | _____ _____ | _____ |

**Capítulo 6A**

Fecha _____ **Vocabulary Flash Cards, Sheet 5**

Copy the word or phrase in the space provided. Be sure to include the article for each noun.

| | | |
|---|---|---|
| **último, última** | **aburrirse** | **enojarse** |
| _____ , _____ | _____ | _____ |
| **volverse loco, loca** | **dormirse** | **morirse** |
| _____ _____ , _____ | _____ | _____ |
| **los campeones** | **competir** | **entrevistar** |
| _____ _____ | _____ | _____ |

Copy the word or phrase in the space provided. These blank cards can be used to write and practice other Spanish vocabulary for the chapter.

| | | |
|---|---|---|
| **ponerse + adjective** <br><br> _____ _____ <br> _____ | | |
| | | |
| | | |

Tear out this page. Write the English words on the lines. Fold the paper along the dotted line to see the correct answers so you can check your work.

aplaudir _____

competir _____

la competencia _____

al final _____

fenomenal _____

resultar _____

último, última _____

el auditorio _____

el comentario _____

entrevistar _____

el público _____

aburrirse _____

alegre _____

emocionado, emocionada _____

enojado, enojada _____

Fold In

**Capítulo 6A**

Fecha _____ **Vocabulary Check, Sheet 2**

Tear out this page. Write the Spanish words on the lines. Fold the paper along the dotted line to see the correct answers so you can check your work.

to applaud _____

to compete _____

competition _____

at the end _____

phenomenal _____

to result, to turn out _____

last, final _____

auditorium _____

commentary _____

to interview _____

audience _____

to get bored _____

happy _____

excited, emotional _____

angry _____

Fold In ←

Tear out this page. Write the English words on the lines. Fold the paper along the dotted line to see the correct answers so you can check your work.

el aficionado,
la aficionada    _____

el atleta, la atleta    _____

el campeonato    _____

el empate    _____

el jugador,
la jugadora    _____

perder    _____

el tanteo    _____

el concurso
de belleza    _____

el premio    _____

la reina    _____

el presentador,
la presentadora    _____

agitado, agitada    _____

furioso, furiosa    _____

dormirse    _____

Fold In

Tear out this page. Write the Spanish words on the lines. Fold the paper along the dotted line to see the correct answers so you can check your work.

fan                    _____

athlete                _____

championship           _____

tie                    _____

player                 _____

to lose                _____

score                  _____

beauty contest         _____

prize                  _____

queen                  _____

presenter              _____

agitated               _____

furious                _____

to fall asleep         _____

Fold In ←

# Preterite of -*ir* stem-changing verbs (p. 302)

- In the preterite, verbs ending in -**ir**, like **preferir**, **pedir**, and **dormir**, have stem changes but only in the **usted/él/ella** and **ustedes/ellos/ellas** forms. The **e** changes to **i**, and the **o** to **u**.

  Mi mamá se d**u**rmió durante la película.
  Mis padres pref**i**rieron ver el concurso de belleza.
  En la liga comp**i**tieron los mejores equipos de México.

- Here are the preterite forms of **preferir**, **pedir**, and **dormir**.

| preferir (e → i) | | pedir (e → i) | | dormir (o → u) | |
|---|---|---|---|---|---|
| preferí | preferimos | pedí | pedimos | dormí | dormimos |
| preferiste | preferisteis | pediste | pedisteis | dormiste | dormisteis |
| **prefirió** | **prefirieron** | **pidió** | **pidieron** | **durmió** | **durmieron** |

**A.** Complete the following sentences by circling the correct form of the verb in parentheses. Then, draw a line beneath the vowel that represents the stem change. The first one is done for you.

1. Carlos ( **prefirió** / prefirieron ) asistir al partido el sábado.

2. Las niñas se ( **durmió** / **durmieron** ) en el auditorio.

3. Usted ( **pidió** / **pedimos** ) una entrevista al entrenador.

4. Ustedes ( **preferiste** / **prefirieron** ) ver este partido.

5. Las presentadoras ( **pidió** / **pidieron** ) a los voluntarios al final del programa.

6. Tomás se ( **durmió** / **dormí** ) antes de la competencia.

7. El campeón ( **pidió** / **pedí** ) un millón de dólares.

8. Lucía ( **preferimos** / **prefirió** ) entrevistar al público.

9. Mis hermanos ( **dormiste** / **durmieron** ) bien anoche.

10. Yo ( **pidieron** / **pedí** ) un café ayer en el café.

# Preterite of *-ir* stem-changing verbs (*continued*)

- Note the special spelling of the preterite forms of **reír**:
  **reí, reíste, rió, reímos, reísteis, rieron**
- Here are other **-ir** verbs with stem changes in the preterite tense:
  Verbs like **preferir: divertirse, mentir, sentirse**
  Verbs like **pedir: competir, despedirse, repetir, seguir, servir, vestirse**
  Verbs like **dormir: morir**
  Verbs like **reír: sonreír**

**B.** Sergio and Patricia went out on a Saturday night. Look at the pictures and fill in the blanks with the correct vowel that represents the stem change. Follow the model.

**Modelo**      Sergio y Patricia se div_i_rtieron mucho.

1. Una tarde, Sergio y Patricia salieron a comer. Ellos s__guieron por la calle Miraflores.

2. Sergio y Patricia p__dieron espaguetis.

3. El camarero les s__rvió una comida muy buena.

4. Después de la cena, Sergio y Patricia pref__rieron ir al cine.

5. Sergio y Patricia se r__eron mucho.

# Preterite of -*ir* stem-changing verbs (*continued*)

**C.** Use the correct form of the verb in parentheses to complete each sentence. The first one is done for you.

1. Millones de aficionados ____*siguieron*____ al jugador. (**seguir**)

2. La reina _____ mucho cuando ganó el concurso de belleza. (**sonreír**)

3. Pilar y yo nos _____ de los chistes que contó el presentador. (**reír**)

4. Al final, la reina de belleza se _____ del público. (**despedirse**)

5. El entrenador y su equipo se _____ de rojo y blanco. (**vestirse**)

6. La presentadora _____ el tanteo para el público. (**repetir**)

7. Ustedes se _____ alegres al final del partido. (**sentirse**)

8. Yo me _____ mucho en el campeonato. (**divertirse**)

9. La reportera dice que el jugador _____; él no rescató a la señora. (**mentir**)

10. Tú no _____ en el campeonato del año pasado. (**competir**)

11. Nosotros _____ una comida fantástica a los jugadores. (**servir**)

12. Ustedes _____ ver el partido en la tele. (**preferir**)

13. Eugenio y tú _____ durante los comentarios. (**dormir**)

14. Yo _____ bebidas para los aficionados sentados cerca de mí. (**pedir**)

15. Resultó que nadie se _____ en el accidente después del partido. (**morir**)

# Other reflexive verbs (p. 305)

• Some reflexive verbs do not have the meaning of a person doing an action to or for himself or herself. These reflexive verbs describe a change. We say that someone "gets" or "becomes" something. Examples of these verbs are:

| aburrirse | to get bored | enojarse | to become angry |
|-----------|--------------|----------|-----------------|
| casarse | to get married | ponerse (furioso, -a; alegre;...) | to become (furious, happy, . . .) |
| divertirse | to have fun | volverse loco, -a | to go crazy |
| dormirse | to fall asleep | | |

**Ramiro se aburrió durante la película.**   *Ramiro got bored during the movie.*
**Lalo se enojó al final del partido.**   *Lalo became angry at the end of the game.*

• Remember that reflexive verbs are used to say that people do something to or for themselves, and they use the reflexive pronouns **me, te, se, os,** and **nos.** Look at the conjugation of the verb **lavarse:**

| yo | **me lavo** | nosotros/nosotras | **nos lavamos** |
|----|-------------|-------------------|-----------------|
| tú | **te lavas** | vosotros/vosotras | **os laváis** |
| usted/él/ella | **se lava** | ustedes/ellos/ellas | **se lavan** |

**A.** Read the following sentences and write the correct reflexive pronoun in the blank. Then, match the meaning of the Spanish verb in the sentences with the English meanings on the right. Follow the model.

**Modelo**   María ___*se*___ casó el domingo. ___*c*___    **a.** went crazy

1. Yo _____ puse alegre con las noticias. _____    **b.** had fun

2. Mis hermanos _____ enojaron cuando su equipo perdió. _____    **c.** got married

3. Nosotros _____ divertimos durante el campeonato. _____    **d.** got bored

4. Juan _____ durmió durante el partido de ayer. _____    **e.** got mad

5. Yo _____ aburrí mucho en el ballet. _____    **f.** became happy

6. Tú _____ volviste loco cuando ganaste. _____    **g.** fell asleep

## Other reflexive verbs (*continued*)

**B.** Circle the verb in parentheses that completes the paragraph. Use the drawings to help you choose which verb to circle. The first one is done for you.

Ayer mi hermano y yo vimos un partido de fútbol en la televisión. Yo

(**me aburrí**/ me volví loco ) mucho porque no me gusta nada el fútbol y mi hermanito

( se casó / **se enojó** ) conmigo. Entonces yo

( me puse furioso / **me divertí** ) y mi hermanito pensó que era muy cómico y

( se aburrió / **se rió** ). El partido de fútbol era muy aburrido y yo

( me puse alegre / **me dormí** ). Cuando me desperté mi hermano no estaba en la sala y

comencé a buscarlo. ( **Me volví loco** / Me divertí ) porque estaba muy

preocupado. Al fin encontré a mi hermanito ¡dormido debajo de su cama! No fue un día

bueno para nosotros y no ( **nos divertimos** / nos casamos ) mucho.

**C.** Complete the sentences telling the changes that took place in the different people. Write the preterite form of the reflexive verb in each sentence.

**Modelo** (**volverse loco**) Felipe __se__ __volvió__ __loco__ cuando su equipo ganó el campeonato.

1. (**casarse**) Mis tíos _____ _____ al final de la estación.

2. (**ponerse furiosos**) Nosotros _____ _____ _____ cuando el equipo perdió por tercera vez contra el mismo equipo.

3. (**divertirse**) Yo _____ _____ en el partido de ayer.

4. (**aburrirse**) Mis primos _____ _____ porque su equipo nunca ganaba.

5. (**ponerse agitada**) Marina _____ _____ _____ con la reina del concurso.

**Capítulo 6A**     Fecha _____     **Guided Practice Activities 6A-5**

# Lectura: Los Juegos Panamericanos (pp. 310–311)

**A.** The reading in your textbook is about the **Juegos Panamericanos** or Pan-American Games, a sports event similar to the Summer Olympics. Using what you already know about the Summer Olympics can help you understand the reading. See if you can answer the questions below.

**1.** What are the Summer Olympics? _____

_____

**2.** Who can participate in the Olympics? _____

**3.** What are five sports often featured in the Summer Olympics? _____,

_____, _____, _____, _____

**B.** Read the following excerpts from your textbook reading. They contain many cognates (words that look and sound like English words) that will help you understand the excerpts. Write what you think some of these words mean in English in the spaces below.

> Los Juegos Panamericanos se establecieron para promover la comprensión entre las naciones del continente americano. Los primeros Juegos se inauguraron el 25 de febrero en 1951 de Buenos Aires, con 2.513 atletas de 22 países.
>
> Todos los países de las Américas pueden mandar atletas a competir. Aproximadamente el 80 por ciento de los deportes de los Juegos Panamericanos se juegan en las Olimpíadas.

**1.** Panamericanos _____     **5.** atletas _____

**2.** se establecieron _____     **6.** Américas _____

**3.** naciones _____     **7.** competir _____

**4.** febrero _____     **8.** Olimpíadas _____

**C.** Now read the sentences below. Based on the excerpts in **part B**, write **Sí** if the sentence tells something that happens during the Pan-American Games. Write **No** if it doesn't happen during the Games.

**1.** Todos los países del mundo pueden participar en estos Juegos. _____

**2.** Las personas que participan en estos Juegos son atletas. _____

**3.** Todos los deportes de los Juegos Panamericanos también se juegan en las

Olimpíadas. _____

# Presentación oral (p. 313)

**Task:** Prepare a review of your favorite television program and present it to your class.

**A.** Complete the following sentences about your favorite television program. Circle one option from the word lists for each sentence and write it in the blank.

| | |
|---|---|
| una comedia | la telenovela |
| un programa deportivo | una película de detectives |
| un programa de concursos | un programa de dibujos animados |

1. Mi programa favorito es _____.

| | | |
|---|---|---|
| niños | mayores | niños y mayores |

2. Este programa es para _____.

| | |
|---|---|
| me río mucho | me enojo mucho |
| me siento emocionado(a) | me vuelvo loco(a) |

3. Cuando veo este programa _____

| | | | |
|---|---|---|---|
| interesante | divertido | fenomenal | alegre |

4. Este programa es _____.

**B.** Now use the information from **part A** to complete the following sentences.

1. Mi programa favorito se llama _____ y es _____

2. Este programa es para _____

3. Cuando veo este programa _____

4. Este programa es _____

**C.** Use the sentences from **parts A** and **B** to practice your oral presentation. Go through the presentation several times. Try to:

- include all the information in the sentences
- use complete sentences and speak clearly

Write the Spanish vocabulary word or phrase below each picture. Be sure to include the article for each noun.

_____

_____

_____

_____

_____

_____

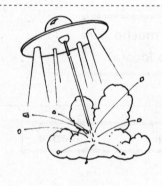

_____

_____

_____

_____

_____

_____

_____

_____

_____

_____

_____

_____

**Capítulo 6B**

Write the Spanish vocabulary word below each picture. If there is a word or phrase, copy it in the space provided. Be sure to include the article for each noun.

el crítico,
la crítica

_____ ,

Nombre _____  Hora _____

Fecha _____  **Vocabulary Flash Cards, Sheet 3**

Copy the word or phrase in the space provided. Be sure to include the article for each noun.

| | | |
|---|---|---|
| **fascinar** <br><br><br> _____ | **el fracaso** <br><br> ____ <br> _____ | **he visto** <br><br> ____ <br> _____ |
| **has visto** <br><br> ____ <br> _____ | **matar** <br><br><br> _____ | **¿Qué tal es...?** <br><br><br> ____ ____ ____ |
| **recomendar** <br><br><br> _____ | **será** <br><br><br> _____ | **tener éxito** <br><br> ____ <br> _____ |

**Capítulo 6B**  Fecha _____  **Vocabulary Flash Cards, Sheet 4**

Copy the word or phrase in the space provided. Be sure to include the article for each noun.

| tratarse de | la violencia | la actuación |
|---|---|---|
| _____ _____ | _____ | _____ |
| el argumento | la dirección | alquilar |
| _____ | _____ | _____ |
| hacer el papel de | el personaje principal | no... todavía |
| _____ _____ | _____ | _____ |

Copy the word or phrase in the space provided. Be sure to include the article for each noun. These blank cards can be used to write and practice other Spanish vocabulary for the chapter.

| | | |
|---|---|---|
| **enamorarse (de)** | **(estar) enamorado, enamorada de** | **el crimen** |
| | _____ | |
| _____ | _____, | |
| _____ | _____ _____ | _____ |
| **la ladrona** | **la escena** | **estar basado, basada en** |
| | | |
| _____ | _____ | _____ _____, |
| _____ | _____ | _____ _____ |
| **el papel** | | |
| | | |
| _____ | _____ | _____ |
| _____ | _____ | _____ |

**Capítulo 6B**

Fecha _____ **Vocabulary Check, Sheet 1**

Tear out this page. Write the English words on the lines. Fold the paper along the dotted line to see the correct answers so you can check your work.

alquilar _____

el amor _____

arrestar _____

capturar _____

el (la) criminal _____

enamorarse (de) _____

robar _____

tener éxito _____

el fracaso _____

tratarse de _____

he visto _____

el director, la directora _____

la escena _____

el papel _____

la víctima _____

Fold In →

Tear out this page. Write the Spanish words on the lines. Fold the paper along the dotted line to see the correct answers so you can check your work.

to rent _____

love _____

to arrest _____

to capture _____

the criminal _____

to fall in love (with) _____

to rob, to steal _____

to succeed, to be successful _____

failure _____

to be about _____

I have seen _____

director _____

scene _____

role _____

victim _____

Fold In

Nombre _____ Hora _____

Fecha _____ **Vocabulary Check, Sheet 3**

Tear out this page. Write the English words on the lines. Fold the paper along the dotted line to see the correct answers so you can check your work.

la estrella (del cine) _____

el (la) detective _____

el galán _____

el ladrón, 
la ladrona _____

la película de 
acción _____

los efectos 
especiales _____

el (la) extraterrestre _____

la actuación _____

el argumento _____

el crimen _____

matar _____

el crítico, la crítica _____

fascinar _____

¿Qué tal es...? _____

Fold In

**Capítulo 6B**     Fecha _____     **Vocabulary Check, Sheet 4**

Tear out this page. Write the Spanish words on the lines. Fold the paper along the dotted line to see the correct answers so you can check your work.

(movie) star     _____

detective        _____

leading man      _____

thief            _____

action film      _____

special effects  _____

alien            _____

acting           _____

plot             _____

crime            _____

to kill          _____

critic           _____

to fascinate     _____

How is (it)...?  _____

Fold In

# Verbs that use indirect object pronouns (p. 328)

- Many verbs that use indirect object pronouns, such as **aburrir, doler, encantar, fascinar, gustar,** and **importar,** use a similar construction:

  indirect object pronoun + verb + subject

  **Le + encantan + las películas de acción.**
  *He likes action movies.*

- You can use **a** + a noun or a pronoun with these verbs for emphasis or to make something clear:

  **A Rodrigo le gustan las flores.**
  *Rodrigo likes flowers.*

  or:

  **A él le gustan las flores.**
  *He likes flowers.*

- Here are the indirect object pronouns:

| (A mí) | **me** | (A nosotros/a nosotras) | **nos** |
|---|---|---|---|
| (A ti) | **te** | (A vosotros/a vosotras) | **os** |
| (A usted/A él/A ella) | **le** | (A ustedes/A ellos/A ellas) | **les** |

**A.** Circle the correct indirect object pronoun to complete each sentence. Follow the model.

**Modelo**   A María ( **le** / les ) encantan las películas románticas.

1. A mí ( **te** / **me** ) aburre este programa.

2. A nosotros ( **nos** / **les** ) molestan los videojuegos.

3. A mi padre y a mí ( **nos** / **te** ) importan los actores de Hollywood.

4. A Pablo y a Ramón ( **le** / **les** ) fascina el cine.

5. A los directores ( **les** / **le** ) encanta trabajar con actores famosos.

6. ¡A ti ( **me** / **te** ) duele la cabeza después de ver tantas películas!

# Verbs that use indirect object pronouns (*continued*)

**B.** In the sentences below, fill in the first blank with the correct indirect object pronoun. Then, write the correct ending for each verb using the words that come after it as clues. Use the pictures to help you guess the correct indirect object pronouns. The first one is done for you.

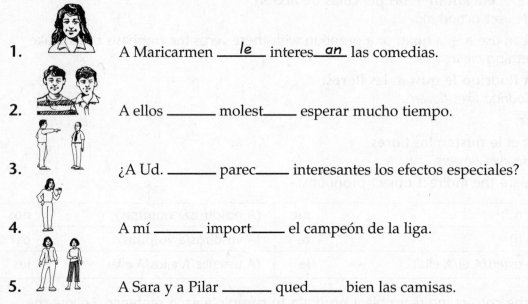

1. A Maricarmen ___*le*___ interes__*an*__ las comedias.

2. A ellos _____ molest_____ esperar mucho tiempo.

3. ¿A Ud. _____ parec_____ interesantes los efectos especiales?

4. A mí _____ import_____ el campeón de la liga.

5. A Sara y a Pilar _____ qued_____ bien las camisas.

**C.** Write questions using the elements given and indirect object pronouns to ask the various people about their entertainment preferences. Follow the model.

**Modelo**   A ti / gustar / ir al cine

¿*A ti te gusta ir al cine* _____ ?

1. A Juan / molestar / las películas de horror

   ¿ _____ ?

2. A Uds. / interesar / los actores

   ¿ _____ ?

3. A Steven Spielberg / importar / la ciencia ficción

   ¿ _____ ?

4. A los criminales / fascinar / las películas de acción

   ¿ _____ ?

5. A mí / parecer / tristes / los dramas

   ¿ _____ ?

**Capítulo 6B**   Fecha _____   **Guided Practice Activities 6B-2**

# The present perfect (p. 331)

Use the present perfect tense to tell what a person has done.

- To form this tense, use present-tense forms of **haber** + the past participle:

  **Hemos alquilado dos películas.**
  *We have rented two movies.*

- To form the past participle of a verb, drop the ending of the infinitive and add **-ado** for **-ar** verbs and **-ido** for **-er** and **-ir** verbs.

|       | alquilar   | vivir  |          | alquilar   | vivir  |
|-------|-----------|--------|----------|-----------|--------|
| he    | alquilado | vivido | **hemos**  | alquilado | vivido |
| has   | alquilado | vivido | **habéis** | alquilado | vivido |
| ha    | alquilado | vivido | **han**    | alquilado | vivido |

**A.** Complete the sentences below with the correct form of the verb **haber**.

**Modelo**  Tú _____*has*_____ vivido en Atlanta, ¿verdad?

1. Mis amigos _____ ido al cine todos los viernes por dos años.

2. Yo nunca _____ alquilado una película de horror.

3. Los directores _____ trabajado mucho en esta película.

4. El actor _____ practicado mucho para este papel.

5. Nosotros _____ oído que es una película muy buena.

- Most verbs that have two vowels together in the infinitive have a written accent on the **í** of the past participle:

  **caer → caído     oír → oído     leer → leído**

**B.** Write the past participle form of the following verbs. Follow the model.

**Modelo**  robar _____*robado*_____

1. matar _____

2. hablar _____

3. perder _____

4. traer _____

5. leer _____

6. aprender _____

7. caer _____

8. oír _____

# The present perfect (*continued*)

**C.** Write the present perfect form of the verb in parentheses in each sentence to tell what things have happened in a recent action movie. Note that in the forms of the present perfect, the past participle does not change; the ending will always be **-o**. Follow the model.

**Modelo**  (**filmar**) El director Mario Fernández ___*ha*___ ___*filmado*___ una nueva película.

1. (**matar**) En la película, unos criminales _____ _____ a algunas personas.

2. (**robar**) Ellos _____ _____ su dinero también.

3. (**esconder**) Un criminal _____ _____ el dinero en el campo.

4. (**capturar**) Los detectives _____ _____ a todos los criminales.

5. (**ir**) Mis amigos y yo _____ _____ al cine a ver la película tres veces.

6. (**leer**) Yo _____ _____ los artículos de los críticos en el periódico.

7. (**crear**) Según los críticos, Fernández _____ _____ efectos especiales fantásticos.

8. (**tener**) Las películas del director Fernández siempre _____ _____ éxito.

9. (**oír**) Y tú, ¿ _____ _____ decir algo bueno sobre esta película?

- These verbs have irregular past participles:

  decir → *dicho*          poner → *puesto*

  escribir → *escrito*     romper → *roto*

  hacer → *hecho*          ver → *visto*

  morir → *muerto*         volver → *vuelto*

**D.** Look at the following verbs. Write **I** (for Irregular) if the verb has an irregular past participle form. If not, write **R** (for Regular). Then, in the second blank, write in the past participle form for each verb, paying close attention to spelling. Follow the model.

**Modelo**  alquilar ___*R*___ ___*alquilado*___

1. volver _____ _____          5. decir _____ _____

2. hacer _____ _____           6. vivir _____ _____

3. escribir _____ _____        7. ver _____ _____

4. comer _____ _____           8. morir _____ _____

# The present perfect (*continued*)

**E.** The following sentences describe a movie. Use the correct form of **haber** plus the past participle of the verb in parentheses to complete the sentences. Follow the model.

Modelo  Yo ____*he*____ ____*visto*____ (**ver**) una película policíaca.

1. El director _____ _____ (**decir**) que el argumento es malo.

2. Nadie _____ _____ (**morir**) en esta escena.

3. Luis y Damián _____ _____ (**hacer**) los papeles de las víctimas.

4. Nosotras _____ _____ (**escribir**) el argumento para la película.

5. ¿Tú _____ _____ (**poner**) el coche en la última escena?

6. La estrella _____ _____ (**romper**) el vaso otra vez.

**F.** Marta is talking about movies. Rewrite her statements by replacing the underlined words with the pronoun in parentheses and placing it before the form of **haber** for each sentence. Follow the model.

Modelo  Yo he alquilado **la película**. (la)

   Yo _____*la he alquilado*_____ .

1. Los detectives han arrestado **a las ladronas**. (las)

   Los detectives _____ .

2. Los actores han leído la escena **al director.** (le)

   Los actores _____ la escena.

3. El galán ha capturado **a los extraterrestres**. (los)

   El galán _____ .

4. El director ha pedido ayuda **a nosotros**. (nos)

   El director _____ ayuda.

5. La directora ha escrito **el argumento**. (lo)

   La directora _____ .

6. El crítico ha dicho su opinión **a mí**. (me)

   El crítico _____ su opinión.

# The present perfect (*continued*)

• When you use object or reflexive pronouns with the present perfect, the pronoun goes right before the form of **haber**:

   **¿Has visto la película? Sí, la he visto.** *Have you seen the movie? Yes, I have seen it.*

**G.** Complete the following sentences by writing the correct reflexive pronoun and the present perfect form of the verbs in parentheses. Use the pictures to help you with meaning. Follow the model. *Note: Some verbs have regular past participles, some require accent marks, and some have irregular past participles.*

**Modelo** (**caerse**) La actriz ___*se*___ ___*ha*___ ___*caído*___.

1. (**volverse**) ¡El director _____ _____ _____ loco!

2. (**enojarse**) Yo _____ _____ _____ muchas veces cuando veo películas de horror.

3. (**casarse**) ¡Qué romántico! Los dos actores famosos _____ _____ _____.

4. (**dormirse**) ¿Tú _____ _____ _____ viendo una película de acción?

5. (**divertirse**) Nosotros _____ _____ _____ viendo las comedias mexicanas.

6. (**vestirse**) Los críticos _____ _____ _____ con elegancia para estos premios.

## Lectura: La cartelera del cine (pp. 336–337)

**A.** First, read the title and subtitles and look at the pictures in the textbook reading. These can give you an idea of what the reading is about or what is the "big picture." Then, circle the best option for the choices below.

1. This reading is about
   **a.** movies.   **b.** sports.   **c.** politics.

2. Each section has a summary and a
   **a.** comedy.   **b.** review.   **c.** drama.

**B.** You will notice that each movie review begins with some basic facts. Read the following fact excerpt from your textbook reading. Then answer the questions below.

*Mad Max: Furia en la carretera*
*Australia, 2015 / Clasificación: R / Director: George Miller / Actores: Tom Hardy, Charlize Theron, Nicholas Hoult, Hugh Keays-Byrne*

1. What is the second part of the title of the movie? _____

2. Who is the director? _____

3. In what year was the movie made? _____

4. What is the classification of the movie? _____

**C.** Read the following *Crítica* or review section for *Los vengadores: La era de Ultrón.* Circle the answer that best completes each of the statements below.

*La película no es más que un anuncio largo para las otras películas de Marvel que se estrenarán en el futuro. El argumento es difícil de seguir, y si bien los efectos especiales son impresionantes, como siempre, hay que trabajar muy duro para seguir la trama complicada y es difícil sentarse y disfrutar de la película.*

1. El crítico de *Los vengadores* piensa que la película es
   **a.** una aventura.   **b.** un anuncio.

2. Al crítico le gustan
   **a.** los efectos especiales.   **b.** los actores.

3. El crítico dice que la película es
   **a.** demasiado corta.   **b.** demasiado complicada.

# Presentación escrita (p. 339)

**Task:** Think about and write a good movie idea for a class contest. Describe the main characters, the plot, and the scenes. Then draw a few scenes from the movie.

**A.** Fill in the blanks with information about the kind of movie you would like to write. You can choose an option from the list, or make up your own.

1. Me gustaría escribir _____.

| | | |
|---|---|---|
| una película de acción | una película romántica | un drama |
| una película de ciencia ficción | una película policíaca | una comedia |
| una película de horror | | |

2. Los personajes principales de mi película pueden ser _____.

| | |
|---|---|
| ladrones y policías | una familia y sus amigos |
| extraterrestres | criminales |

**B.** Read the following plot descriptions to get ideas for your movie. You can use these descriptions or make up your own. Then write a brief outline of your plot below.

- Los personajes desean encontrar algo que alguien escondió hace muchos años.
- Los extraterrestres vienen a visitarnos.
- Unos ladrones roban una pintura *(painting)* de un museo y la policía los busca.

_____
_____
_____
_____

**C.** In the following boxes, sketch four scenes from the movie plot you described in **part B**.

# A ver si recuerdas: Verbs with irregular *yo* forms (p. 345)

- As you know, some verbs have irregular **yo** forms in the present tense. These fall into two categories:

  Verbs with irregular **-go** forms:

  | | | |
  |---|---|---|
  | salir → yo salgo | poner → yo pongo | hacer → yo hago |
  | caer → yo caigo | decir → yo digo | venir → yo vengo |

  Verbs with irregular **-zco** forms:

  | | |
  |---|---|
  | conocer → yo conozco | parecer → yo parezco |
  | obedecer → yo obedezco | ofrecer → yo ofrezco |

**A.** Change the following verbs from the **tú** form to the **yo** form. Follow the model.

Modelo   pones    _____*pongo*_____

1. sales    _____

2. conoces    _____

3. dices    _____

4. ofreces    _____

5. obedeces    _____

6. caes    _____

7. haces    _____

8. vienes    _____

**B.** Elena is living with her aunt and uncle for the summer. Complete her e-mail by writing the **yo** form of the verbs given. The first one is done for you.

Estimada Mónica:

¿Cómo estás? Yo estoy muy bien aquí con mis tíos, pero yo

_____*tengo*_____ (**tener**) mucho trabajo. Yo me levanto

y _____ _____ (**ponerse**) la ropa muy temprano.

Después, yo _____ (**salir**) de la casa para

trabajar con mi tío. Yo siempre _____ (**hacer**) lo

que él necesita y yo nunca le _____ (**decir**) que

estoy cansada. ¡Es trabajo divertido!

⟶

# A ver si recuerdas: Verbs with irregular *yo* forms (*continued*)

Bueno, yo ya _____ (**conocer**) a muchas personas

del pueblo. ¡Todos dicen que yo _____ _____

(**parecerse**) mucho a mi tío! Al final del día, cuando

_____ (**venir**) a la casa, siempre le

_____ (**ofrecer**) un poco de ayuda a mi tía, que

está preparando la cena. En total, yo _____

(**tener**) una vida muy interesante aquí.

Un abrazo,

Elena

**C.** Answer the following questions in complete sentences, paying special attention to the verbs with irregular **yo** forms.

Modelo   ¿Siempre dices la verdad?

   Sí, yo siempre _____*digo la verdad*_____.

1. ¿Te pareces a alguien de tu familia?

   Sí, yo _____ a mi _____.

2. ¿Siempre obedeces a tus padres?

   No, yo no _____ siempre.

3. ¿A veces sales por la noche con tus amigos?

   Sí, yo _____ a veces _____.

4. ¿Conoces a alguna persona famosa?

   No, no _____.

5. ¿Tienes mucha tarea esta noche?

   Sí, yo _____.

6. ¿Haces la tarea por la tarde o por la noche?

   Yo _____.

| Nombre | Hora |
|---|---|

**Capítulo 7A**

Fecha

**Vocabulary Flash Cards, Sheet 1**

Write the Spanish vocabulary word below each picture. Be sure to include the article for each noun.

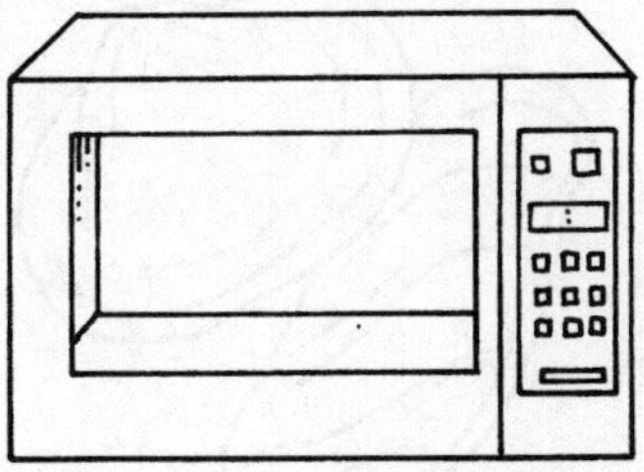

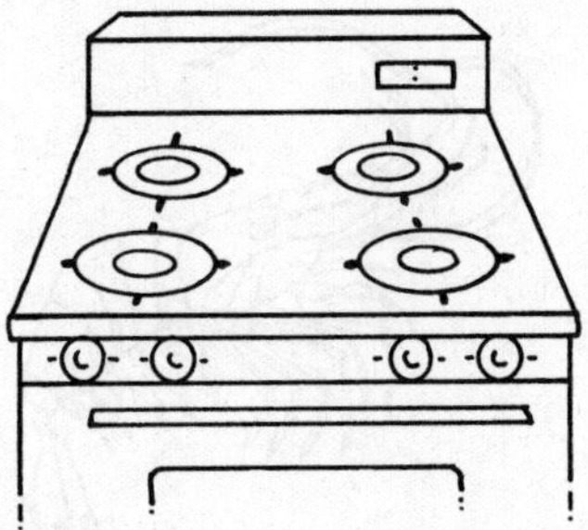

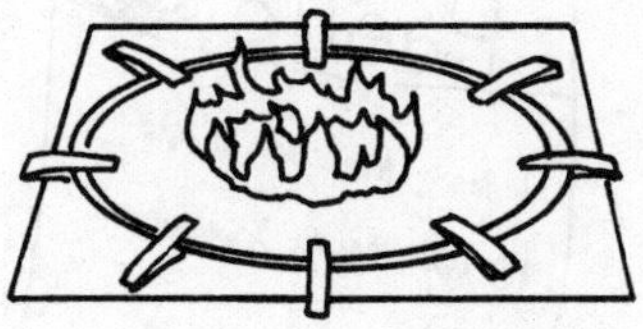

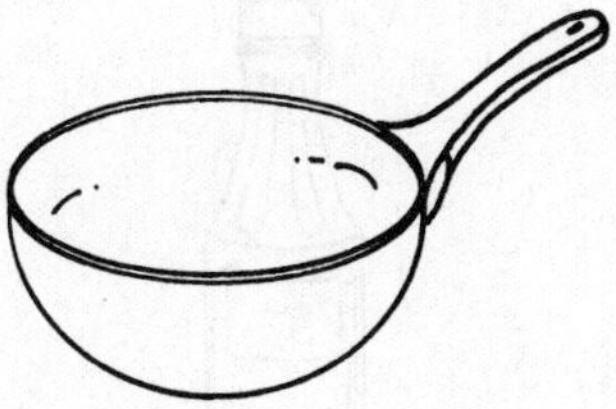

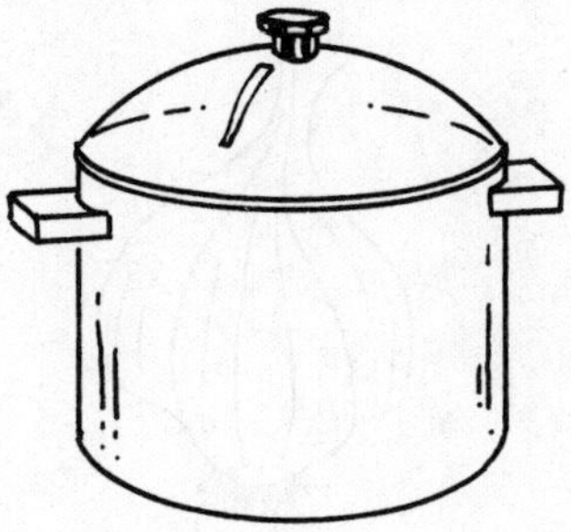

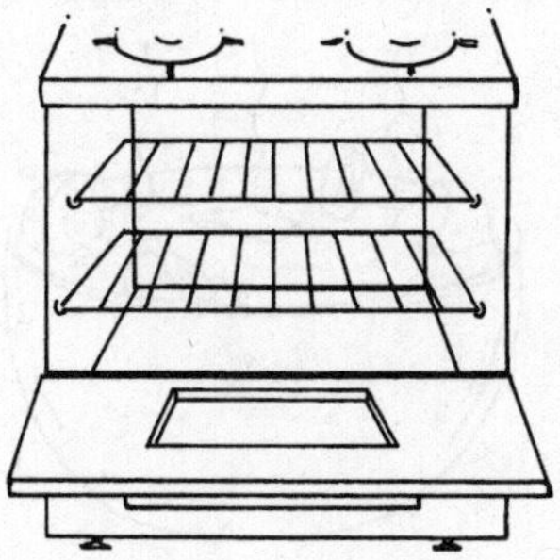

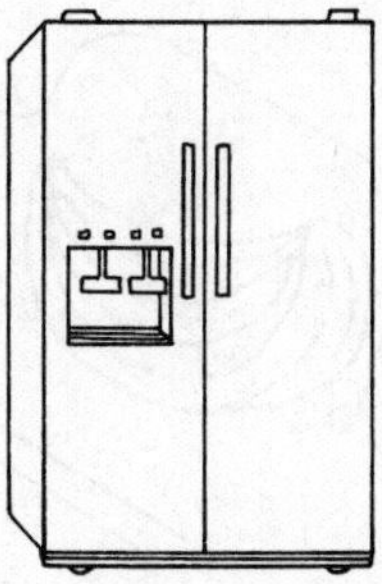

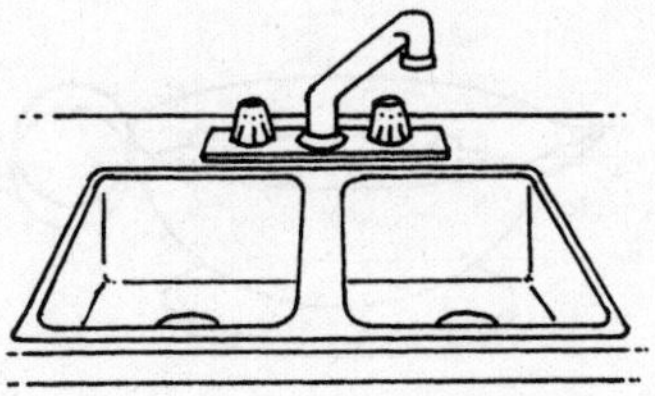

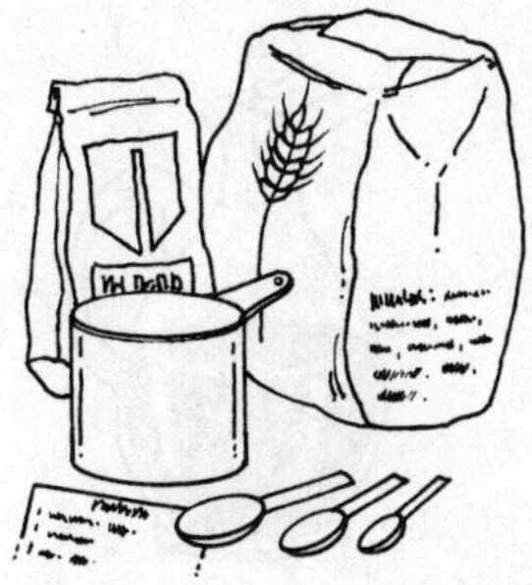

Write the Spanish vocabulary word below each picture. Be sure to include the article for each noun.

_____

_____

_____

_____

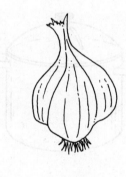

_____

_____

_____

_____

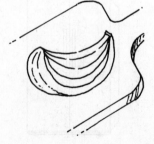

_____

Write the Spanish vocabulary word below each picture. Be sure to include the article for each noun.

Write the Spanish vocabulary word below each picture. If there is a word or phrase, copy it in the space provided.

_____

_____

_____

_____

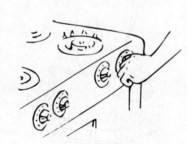

_____

**frito, frita**

_____,

**¿Cómo se hace...?**

_____

_____

**¿Con qué se sirve?**

_____

_____

**no añadas**

_____

_____

**Capítulo 7A**

Fecha _____

Copy the word or phrase in the space provided. Be sure to include the article for each noun.

| | | |
|---|---|---|
| **dejar** | **no dejes** | **olvidarse de** |
| _____ | _____ | _____ |
| **no te olvides de** | **no tires** | **se puede** |
| _____ _____ | _____ | _____ |
| **No hables.** | **No comas.** | **No escribas.** |
| _____ | _____ | _____ |

**Capítulo 7A**

Copy the word or phrase in the space provided. These blank cards can be used to write and practice other Spanish vocabulary for the chapter.

| | | |
|---|---|---|
| **congelado, congelada** | **enlatado, enlatada** | **fresco, fresca** |
| _____, _____ | _____, _____ | _____, _____ |

Tear out this page. Write the English words on the lines. Fold the paper along the dotted line to see the correct answers so you can check your work.

la salsa _____

el aceite _____

el ajo _____

la olla _____

el refrigerador _____

el fuego _____

caliente _____

el horno _____

añadir _____

tirar _____

freír _____

mezclar _____

probar _____

la receta _____

olvidarse de _____

Fold In

Tear out this page. Write the Spanish words on the lines. Fold the paper along the dotted line to see the correct answers so you can check your work.

salsa, sauce _____

cooking oil _____

garlic _____

pot _____

refrigerator _____

fire, heat _____

hot _____

oven _____

to add _____

to spill, to
throw away _____

to fry _____

to mix _____

to taste, to try _____

recipe _____

to forget about/to _____

Fold In ←

Tear out this page. Write the English words on the lines. Fold the paper along the dotted line to see the correct answers so you can check your work.

el caldo _____

la estufa _____

el fregadero _____

el pedazo _____

la sartén _____

calentar _____

hervir _____

el ingrediente _____

picar _____

apagar _____

dejar _____

encender _____

fresco, fresca _____

Fold In →

**Capítulo 7A**

Fecha _____  **Vocabulary Check, Sheet 4**

Tear out this page. Write the Spanish words on the lines. Fold the paper along the dotted line to see the correct answers so you can check your work.

broth _____

stove _____

sink _____

piece, slice _____

frying pan _____

to heat _____

to boil _____

ingredient _____

to chop _____

to turn off _____

to leave, to let _____

to turn on, to light _____

fresh _____

Fold In →

## Capítulo 7A

# Negative *tú* commands (p. 356)

- Negative commands are used to tell someone what *not* to do.
- To form negative **tú** commands, drop the **-o** of the present-tense **yo** form and add:
  **-es** for **-ar** verbs
    **usar → uso: No uses el microondas.** *Don't use the microwave.*
  **-as** for **-er** and **-ir** verbs
    **encender → enciendo: No enciendas el horno.** *Don't turn on the oven.*

**A.** Look at the following sentences and add the correct endings to the verbs to make negative **tú** commands. Use the verbs in parentheses for reference. Follow the model.

**Modelo**  Jaime, no com _as_ todas las frutas. (**comer**)

1. Raquel, no tir_____ el pollo en el aceite caliente. (**tirar**)

2. Tadeo, no cort_____ el ajo en pedazos tan pequeños. (**cortar**)

3. Susana, no beb_____ el café si está muy caliente. (**beber**)

4. Mario, no us_____ tanto aceite en el sartén. (**usar**)

5. Julia, no añad_____ el ajo ahora. (**añadir**)

- Remember that some verbs have irregular **yo** forms, which are used to form the negative commands.
    **salir → salgo    No salga de la casa.**    *Don't leave the house.*

**B.** Complete the statements below by writing the correct negative **tú** commands of the verbs given. Follow the model.

**Modelo**  (**poner**) _____ *No pongas* _____ las manos en la masa.

1. (**salir**) _____ sin comer algo.

2. (**decir**) _____ mentiras (*lies*).

3. (**hacer**) _____ eso, por favor.

4. (**obedecer**) _____ a tus amigos malos.

# Negative *tú* commands (*continued*)

- Remember that stem-changing verbs will still have the same stem changes to form the negative commands. Also, if the verb is reflexive, the reflexive pronoun will be placed the same way.

  **dormirse → te duermas**

  **¡No te duermas en la clase!**    *Don't fall asleep in class!*

**C.** Look at the following verbs in the infinitive. Write the negative command form for each. Follow the model.

**Modelo**  divertirse  ___*No te diviertas.*___

1. encender _____
2. calentar _____
3. probar _____
4. hervir _____

5. caerse _____
6. parecerse _____
7. olvidarse _____
8. dormirse _____

- With negative **tú** commands, some verbs such as **picar** (*to chop*), **pagar** (*to pay*), and **empezar** (*to start*) have spelling changes: **c** changes to **qu**, **g** changes to **gu**, and **z** changes to **c**.

  **picar → no pi**qu**es**    **pagar → no pa**gu**es**    **empezar → no empie**c**es**

**D.** Your parents have given you a list of things not to do on the weekend. Complete their list by writing the correct negative **tú** commands of the verbs given. Follow the model.

**Modelo**  ___No___  ___empieces___  la tarea a las nueve de la noche los domingos.
              **(empezar)**

1. _____  _____ en restaurantes caros. **(almorzar)**
2. _____  _____ problemas en la calle. **(buscar)**
3. _____  _____ con las personas malas. **(jugar)**
4. _____  _____ a casa después de las diez de la noche. **(llegar)**
5. _____  _____ cosas de la casa de otra persona sin pedirlas. **(sacar)**

# Negative *tú* commands (*continued*)

- Some verbs have irregular negative **tú** commands:

  **dar → no des**    **estar → no estés**
  **ir → no vayas**    **ser → no seas**

**E.** For each of the following sentences, write the appropriate negative **tú** command of the verb in parentheses.

1. No _____ (**dar**) dulces a tu hermano antes del almuerzo.

2. No _____ (**estar**) en la cocina antes de la cena.

3. No _____ (**ir**) al mercado hoy.

4. No _____ (**ser**) tan desordenada.

- Remember that pronouns are attached to the verb when they are added to the affirmative command form. Note: An accent mark is written on the verb when the added pronoun makes three or more syllables.

  —**¿Añado la sal?**    *Do I add the salt?*
  —**Sí, añádela.**    *Yes, add it.*

**F.** Read the following questions and unfinished answers. Place the correct pronoun in the spaces provided to finish the answers. Remember to add an accent, if necessary, to the affirmative command in each answer. Follow the model.

Modelo   —¿Mezclo los ingredientes en la taza?

      —Sí, mézcla _los_ en la taza.

1. —¿Añado el aceite a la sartén?

   —Sí, añáde_____ a la sartén.

2. —¿Tiro los huesos del pollo?

   —Sí, tíra_____.

3. —¿Apago el fuego de la estufa?

   —Sí, apága_____.

4. —¿Pongo la mesa antes de la cena?

   —Sí, pon_____ antes de la cena.

5. —¿Saco los platos después de la comida?

   —Sí, sáca_____ después de la comida.

# Negative *tú* commands (*continued*)

- Pronouns always go right before the verb when writing negative commands.

   —¿Pongo los platos en la mesa?
   *Should I put the plates on the table?*

   —No, no *los pongas* en la mesa en este momento.
   *No, don't put them on the table right now.*

**G.** Señor Báez is giving a class on cooking. Nacho is having trouble with many of the tasks. Follow the conversation below by writing in señor Báez' responses using negative **tú** commands. Remember to correctly place the pronouns in each. The first one is done for you.

1. NACHO:      ¿Debo apagar el horno?

   SEÑOR BÁEZ:   No, _____*no lo apagues*_____.

2. NACHO:      ¿Debo hacer el arroz?

   SEÑOR BÁEZ:   No, _____.

3. NACHO:      ¿Debo pelar los tomates?

   SEÑOR BÁEZ:   No, _____.

4. NACHO:      ¿Debo picar los huevos?

   SEÑOR BÁEZ:   No, _____.

5. NACHO:      ¿Debo freír la ensalada?

   SEÑOR BÁEZ:   No, _____.

6. NACHO:      ¿Debo poner el pan en el microondas?

   SEÑOR BÁEZ:   No, _____ allí.

7. NACHO:      ¿Debo mezclar la leche con los tomates?

   SEÑOR BÁEZ:   No, _____ con los tomates.

8. NACHO:      ¿Debo hervir los huevos en la sartén?

   SEÑOR BÁEZ:   No, _____ en la sartén.

# The impersonal *se* (p. 360)

- In Spanish, to say that people in general do a certain thing, you use **se** + the **usted/él/ella** or **ustedes/ellos/ellas** form of the verb. This is called the impersonal **se**.

    **Aquí se sirve el pan tostado con mantequilla.** *Here they serve the toast with butter.*
    **Se comen tortillas frecuentemente.** *Tortillas are eaten frequently.*

**A.** Look at the pictures and read the sentences that describe what people do in general when they prepare food. Circle the appropriate impersonal **se** expression in parentheses to complete each sentence.

1. En mi casa el pollo ( **se hace** / **se tira** ) con sal y ajo.

2. Para preparar la salsa ( **se calienta** / **se pica** ) el ajo.

3. El plato principal ( **se sirve** / **se hierve** ) con ensalada.

4. En mi casa ( **se come** / **se bebe** ) mucha fruta.

5. La comida ( **se pica** / **se calienta** ) en el microondas.

# The impersonal *se* (*continued*)

- Note: The **usted/él/ella form** of the verb is used when the thing following it is singular and the **ustedes/ellos/ellas** form is used when the thing following it is plural.

  | | |
  |---|---|
  | **Se pela la papa.** | *The potato is pealed.* |
  | **Se pelan las papas.** | *The potatoes are pealed.* |

**B.** Complete the following rules by circling the appropriate impersonal **se** expression to tell what is done or not done. Follow the model.

**Modelo**     No ( (se fríen) / se fríe ) los camarones.

1. ( Se sirven / Se sirve ) pan con mariscos.

2. ( Se calienta / Se calientan ) el pan en el horno.

3. No ( se añade / se añaden ) sal a la sopa.

4. ( Se dejan / Se deja ) el ajo en la cocina.

5. No ( se hierve / se hierven ) los mariscos.

**C.** Complete the following recipe to prepare **arroz con mariscos**. Use the impersonal **se** form of the verb in parentheses to complete each instruction. The first one is done for you. Be careful to choose between the singular and plural verb forms.

**Arroz con mariscos**

1. _____*Se calienta*_____ (**calentar**) el aceite en la sartén.

2. _____ (**preparar**) los mariscos con sal.

3. _____ (**pelar**) el ajo y

4. _____ (**cortar**) en pedazos.

5. _____ (**mezclar**) los mariscos y el ajo.

6. _____ (**hervir**) agua en una olla.

7. _____ (**añadir**) arroz y sal al caldo.

8. _____ (**mezclar**) los mariscos con el arroz.

# Lectura: "Oda al tomate" y "Oda a la cebolla" (pp. 364–365)

**A.** The two poems in your textbook reading are about tomatoes and onions. What words would you use to describe a tomato or an onion? Write them below.

tomato: _____, _____, _____

onion: _____, _____, _____, _____

**B.** These poems use many descriptive words to tell us about tomatoes and onions. Some of these words are listed below. Circle the letter of the English meaning of each word.

1. **redonda**        **a.** small        **b.** round

2. **clara**          **a.** clear        **b.** dark

3. **pobres**         **a.** rich         **b.** poor

4. **constelación**   **a.** condition    **b.** constellation

5. **planeta**        **a.** planet       **b.** plantation

**C.** Look at the excerpt of **"Oda a la cebolla"** below. Read it aloud and look back at your answers from **part B** if you need help with the meaning of certain words. Then, write **C (cierto)** or **F (falso)** for each sentence below.

> (...) cebolla,
> clara como un planeta,
> y destinada
> a relucir (shine),
> constelación constante,
> redonda (round) rosa
> de agua sobre la mesa
> de las pobres gentes.

1. According to the poet, the onion is like a planet. _____

2. An onion is also like a tomato. _____

3. *Redonda rosa de agua* means that it is like a white flower. _____

4. The poet says that everyone has an onion on their table. _____

**Capítulo 7A**

# Presentación oral (p. 367)

**Task:** Imagine you are a guest on a television cooking show. You will be telling the audience how to prepare your favorite main dish.

**A.** Write the name of your favorite dish below. Then place an *X* next to the ingredients in the chart that you need to prepare that dish.

**Mi plato favorito es** _____ .

| Ingredientes | | | |
|---|---|---|---|
| ____ huevos | ____ caldo | ____ carne | ____ tomate |
| ____ agua | ____ pollo | ____ lechuga | ____ ajo |
| ____ leche | ____ sal | ____ cebolla | ____ pimienta |
| ____ camarones | ____ queso | ____ aceite | ____ mariscos |

**B.** Use the ingredients you chose in **part A**. Think about the steps you would follow to prepare your dish. You can use the verbs for food preparation from the list or others you have learned in this chapter.

| se mezcla | se corta | se sirve | se pone | se añade |
|---|---|---|---|---|

Now, complete the recipe card below. Include the name of the dish, the ingredients you need, and the steps to prepare this dish.

**Nombre del plato:** _____

**Ingredientes:** _____

**Preparación:** _____

   **1.** Primero, _____

   **2.** Luego, _____

   **3.** Después, _____

   **4.** Al final, _____

**C.** Use your recipe card to practice your presentation. Remember to include the ingredients, describe the steps to prepare the dish, and to speak clearly.

**Capítulo 7B**

**Vocabulary Flash Cards, Sheet 1**

Write the Spanish vocabulary word or phrase below each picture. Be sure to include the article for each noun.

Write the Spanish vocabulary word or phrase below each picture. Be sure to include the article for each noun.

_____

_____

_____

_____

_____

_____

_____

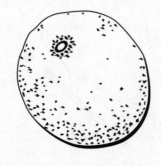

_____

_____

**Capítulo 7B**   Fecha _____   **Vocabulary Flash Cards, Sheet 3**

Write the Spanish vocabulary word or phrase below each picture. Be sure to include the article for each noun.

Write the Spanish vocabulary word below each picture. If there is a word or phrase, copy it in the space provided. Be sure to include the article for each noun.

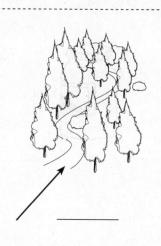

_____

_____

_____

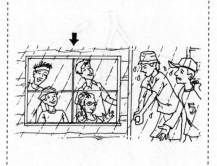

_____ ,

_____

_____ ,

_____

**asado, asada**

_____ ,

_____

**fuera (de)**

_____

**dentro de**

_____

**el cielo**

_____

**Capítulo 7B**     Fecha _____     **Vocabulary Flash Cards, Sheet 5**

Copy the word or phrase in the space provided. Be sure to include the article for each noun. These blank cards can be used to write and practice other Spanish vocabulary for the chapter.

| | | |
|---|---|---|
| **la harina** _____ _____ | **dulce** _____ | **grasoso, grasosa** _____, _____ |
| **acompañar** _____ | **al aire libre** ____ ____ _____ | **el suelo** ____ _____ |
| **el sabor** _____ _____ | | |

These blank cards can be used to write and practice other Spanish vocabulary for
the chapter.

Tear out this page. Write the English words on the lines. Fold the paper along the dotted line to see the correct answers so you can check your work.

al aire libre _____

el cielo _____

dentro de _____

fuera (de) _____

la nube _____

la piedra _____

el aguacate _____

la chuleta de cerdo _____

los frijoles _____

la harina _____

el maíz _____

el sabor _____

dulce _____

picante _____

acompañar _____

Fold In

**Capítulo 7B**

Tear out this page. Write the Spanish words on the lines. Fold the paper along the dotted line to see the correct answers so you can check your work.

outdoors _____

sky _____

inside _____

outside _____

cloud _____

rock _____

avocado _____

pork chop _____

beans _____

flour _____

corn _____

taste _____

sweet _____

spicy _____

to accompany _____

Fold In →

**Capítulo 7B**

Tear out this page. Write the English words on the lines. Fold the paper along the dotted line to see the correct answers so you can check your work.

el sendero _____

el suelo _____

la fogata _____

el fósforo _____

la leña _____

a la parrilla _____

el puesto _____

asado, asada _____

asar _____

la carne de res _____

la cereza _____

la cesta _____

la mayonesa _____

la mostaza _____

Fold In

Tear out this page. Write the Spanish words on the lines. Fold the paper along the dotted line to see the correct answers so you can check your work.

trail                    _____

ground, floor            _____

bonfire                  _____

match                    _____

firewood                 _____

on the grill             _____

(food) stand             _____

grilled                  _____

to grill, to roast       _____

steak                    _____

cherry                   _____

basket                   _____

mayonnaise               _____

mustard                  _____

Fold In

**Capítulo 7B**

# Usted and ustedes commands (p. 382)

- Use the **usted** command form to tell someone older than you what to do or what *not* to do. Use the **ustedes** form to tell a group of people what to do or what *not* to do.

  **Coma Ud. el arroz.     Beban Uds. la leche.**

- **-ar** verbs use **-e** for **Ud.** commands, and **-en** for **Uds.** commands; **-er** and **-ir** verbs use **-a** for **Ud.** commands, and **-an** for **Uds.** commands.

- The commands for **viajar**, **comer**, and **servir** are shown below.

| verbs ending in *-ar* | | | verbs ending in *-er* | | | verbs ending in *-ir* | | |
|---|---|---|---|---|---|---|---|---|
| **viajar** | **usted** | **ustedes** | **comer** | **usted** | **ustedes** | **servir** | **usted** | **ustedes** |
| yo viaj**o** | viaj**e** | viaj**en** | yo com**o** | com**a** | com**an** | yo sirv**o** | sirv**a** | sirv**an** |

**A.** Write the correct ending for the **usted** or **ustedes** command form for each of the infinitives below. The first one is done for you.

1. abrir      abr _an_ Uds.

2. batir      bat_____ Ud.

3. calentar   calient_____ Ud.

4. entrar     entr_____ Uds.

5. añadir     añad_____ Uds.

6. tirar      tir_____ Ud.

7. hervir     hierv_____ Uds.

8. pelar      pel_____ Ud.

**B.** Write the correct **usted** or **ustedes** command form for each sentence using the verbs in parentheses. Follow the model.

**Modelo**   (hervir)  No _____ *hierva* _____ Ud. el agua.

1. (cortar)     No _____ Ud. los huevos.

2. (preparar)   No _____ Uds. el desayuno.

3. (freír)      No _____ Uds. el pescado.

4. (probar)     No _____ Ud. el tocino.

5. (encender)   No _____ Ud. el horno.

# *Usted* and *ustedes* commands (*continued*)

- Affirmative and negative **usted** and **ustedes** commands have the same spelling changes and irregular forms as the negative **tú** commands:

| (hacer) | Haga Ud. | Hagan Uds. |
|---------|----------|------------|
| (buscar) | Busque Ud. | Busquen Uds. |
| (almorzar) | Almuerce Ud. | Almuercen Uds. |

**C.** Write the correct **usted/ustedes** command for each verb in parentheses. Follow the model.

Modelo   (poner) _____*Pongan*_____ Uds. los platos en el fregadero.

1. (hacer)      _____ Uds. un picnic para sus amigos.

2. (picar)   No _____ Ud. el durazno.

3. (buscar)  No _____ Ud. la fogata sin leña.

4. (tener)      _____ Ud. cuidado con las hormigas.

5. (almorzar)  No _____ Uds. sin vasos.

- If you want to use a pronoun such as **lo, la, los,** or **las** with an affirmative command, attach it to the end of the command. You will need to add a written accent mark in the commands.

    —**¿Dónde ponemos la leña?** *Where do we put the firewood?*

    —**Pónganla en un lugar seco.** *Put it in a dry place.*

**D.** Rewrite the following commands, replacing the underlined words with pronouns (**lo, la, los,** or **las**). Remember to add written accents where necessary. Follow the model.

Modelo   Preparen <u>la comida</u>.          _____*Prepárenla*_____ .

1. Compre <u>las hamburguesas</u>.      _____ .

2. Traigan <u>los frijoles</u>.      _____ .

3. Busque <u>la leña</u>.      _____ .

4. Asen <u>el pollo</u>.      _____ .

5. Piquen <u>los tomates</u>.      _____ .

6. Coma <u>las galletas</u>.      _____ .

## *Usted* and *ustedes* commands (*continued*)

- If you want to use a pronoun with a negative command, put it right before the command.
  - **—¿Encendemos la fogata?** *Should we light the fire?*
  - **—No, no la enciendan.** *No, don't light it.*

**E.** Eugenia and señora López are discussing some things students shouldn't do when camping. Fill in señora López's responses with the correct **usted/ustedes** command forms of the verbs in parentheses. The first one is done for you.

1. EUGENIA:  ¿Lavamos las ollas aquí? (**lavar**)

   SEÑORA LÓPEZ: No, _____*no los laven*_____ allí.

2. EUGENIA:  ¿Traemos la mostaza para encender el fuego? (**traer**)

   SEÑORA LÓPEZ: No, _____ para encender el fuego.

3. EUGENIA:  ¿Sacamos los fósforos ahora? (**sacar**)

   SEÑORA LÓPEZ: No, _____ ahora.

4. EUGENIA:  ¿Buscamos un parque en la ciudad para la fogata? (**buscar**)

   SEÑORA LÓPEZ: No, _____ en la ciudad.

5. EUGENIA:  ¿Servimos las chuletas luego? (**servir**)

   SEÑORA LÓPEZ: No, _____ luego.

6. EUGENIA:  ¿Dejamos los fósforos en el bosque? (**dejar**)

   SEÑORA LÓPEZ: No, _____ en el bosque.

# Uses of *por* (p. 386)

The preposition **por** is used in many ways.

- To tell about time or distance: **Yo dormí por ocho horas.** *I slept for eight hours.*
- To tell about movement: **Vamos a caminar por el sendero.** *Let's walk along the path.*
- To tell about exchanging one thing for another: **No pagué mucho por la piña.**
  *I didn't pay much for the pineapple.*
- To tell about a reason: **Yo fui al mercado por unas cerezas.** *I went to the market for some cherries.*
- To tell about an action on someone's behalf: **Encendí la parrilla por Luisa.** *I lit the grill for Luisa.*
- To tell about a way of communication or transportation: **¿Vas a viajar por avión?**
  *Are you going to travel by plane?*

**A.** Choose the best ending from the word bank to complete each sentence below. Use the context clues given to help you decide. Follow the model.

| por avión | ~~por tres horas~~ | por la leche | por el sendero | por mis padres |

**Modelo** Nosotros preparamos la cena _____ *por tres horas* _____.
(*how much time?*)

1. Vamos a viajar _____.
   (*what form of transportation?*)

2. Voy a cocinar _____.
   (*on whose behalf?*)

3. Tú vas a caminar _____.
   (*how did you move?*)

4. Voy a la tienda _____.
   (*for what?*)

**B.** Each of these sentences below ends with an expression that uses **por**. Write the letter of the best ending for each sentence.

1. Yo dormí _____.
   **a.** por la camisa   **b.** por dos horas

2. Lupe va a la tienda _____.
   **a.** por avión   **b.** por el periódico

3. Me gusta viajar _____.
   **a.** por dos tomates   **b.** por avión

4. ¿Cuánto dinero pagaste _____?
   **a.** por el sendero   **b.** por esa piña

5. Voy a preparar la carne _____.
   **a.** por mi hermano   **b.** por teléfono

## Lectura: El Yunque (pp. 390–391)

**A.** Your textbook reading is about a national park called **El Yunque.** What kind of things do you think you'll read about in the reading? Add two more questions to the list about things you think the reading may describe.

¿Dónde está el parque? ¿Qué hay en el parque? ¿Qué tipos de plantas hay?

_____, _____

**B.** Read the following selections from the reading about **El Yunque.** As you read, find answers to some of the questions in **part A** and write them below.

> *El Yunque es una de las atracciones más visitadas de Puerto Rico. . . .*
> *Más de 240 especies de árboles coexisten con animales exóticos, como*
> *el coquí y la boa de Puerto Rico.*
>
> *La mejor forma de explorar este parque es caminando por las varias*
> *veredas (paths) que pasan por el bosque.*

**1.** ¿Dónde está el parque? El parque ésta en _____.

**2.** ¿Qué hay en el parque? Hay _____

_____.

**3.** ¿Qué tipos de plantas hay? Hay _____.

**C.** Look at the following advice from the reading about walking in **El Yunque.** After you read the selection, place a ✓ next to those sentences that are true.

> *Consejos para el caminante*
> *1 Nunca camine solo. Siempre vaya acompañado.*
> *2 Traiga agua y algo para comer.*
> *3 Use repelente para insectos.*
> *4 No abandone las veredas para no perderse (to get lost).*
> *5 No toque (touch) las plantas del bosque.*

**1.** Never walk alone in the park. _____

**2.** Don't take food or water with you. _____

**3.** Use insect repellent. _____

**4.** Don't walk along the paths. _____

**5.** Touch the plants in the forest. _____

# Presentación escrita (p. 393)

**Task:** You will write and illustrate a poster on safety and fun at an outdoor cookout.

**A.** Read and circle the sentences below that tell about something you need for an outdoor cookout.

1. Se necesitan fósforos.

2. Se debe comprar carne.

3. Se debe buscar un lugar mojado.

4. Se necesita leña.

5. Se debe llevar regla y lápiz.

6. Se debe comprar agua o refrescos.

7. Se debe mirar una película.

**B.** Now, read and circle the commands below that provide good advice before, during, and after a cookout.

1. Tengan cuidado con la parrilla caliente.

2. Lleven sus videojuegos.

3. Compren carne para asar.

4. Busquen un lugar seco para hacer la fogata.

5. Lleven repelente para mosquitos.

6. No jueguen cerca de un lago.

7. No tiren nada en el parque.

8. No apaguen la fogata antes de salir.

**C.** Using your answers from **parts A** and **B**, write a short paragraph. Mention how to stay safe and have fun before, during, and after the cookout. You may use the sentence starters below.

*Antes de hacer una parrillada, ustedes necesitan* _____.

*El lugar debe* _____.

*Para hacer la fogata deben* _____.

*No jueguen ustedes con* _____.

*Antes de salir,* _____.

**D.** Review the spelling and vocabulary on your poster. Check that your paragraph includes the appropriate commands and is easy to understand.

**E.** Use artwork to illustrate your sentences on the poster.

## A ver si recuerdas: The infinitive in verbal expressions (p. 399)

- Many verbal expressions contain infinitives. These include:

  Expressing plans, desires, and wishes:

  > **Mi hermana *piensa nadar* pero yo *quiero pasear* en bote.**
  > *My sister is thinking of swimming but I want to take a boat ride.*

  Expressing obligation:

  > **¿*Tienes que descansar* ahora?**
  > *Do you have to rest now?*

- In these expressions, only the first verb is conjugated. The second verb remains in the infinitive. Consider these sentences:

  > **Mi hermana nada y pasea en bote.**
  > *My sister swims and takes boat rides.*

  > **Mi hermana *piensa nadar* y *quiere pasear* en bote también.**
  > *My sister is thinking of swimming and wants to take a boat ride, too.*

**A.** Read the following sentences. Circle the correct verb from the parentheses. Follow the models.

**Modelo 1** Julia y Ramón ( (van) / ir ) de pesca a menudo.

**Modelo 2** Mi tía y yo queremos ( vamos / (ir) ) al cine.

1. A nosotros nos gustaría ( tomamos / **tomar** ) el sol.

2. Mi padre prefiere ( **esquiar** / esquía ).

3. Todas las tardes, yo ( **monto** / montar ) a caballo.

4. ¿Piensas tú ( vas / **ir** ) de cámping?

5. Yo debo ( **comprar** / compro ) recuerdos para mi familia.

6. Mis amigos ( **toman** / tomar ) muchas fotos.

7. ¿Quieres ( **ir** / vas ) a las montañas con nosotros?

8. Juan y yo tenemos que ( **regresar** / regresamos ) al hotel ahora.

# A ver si recuerdas: The infinitive in verbal expressions (*continued*)

- The infinitive is also used after impersonal verbal expressions:

  ***Es necesario tener* mucho cuidado cuando buceas.**
  *It is necessary to be very careful when you scuba dive.*

  ***Hay que regresar* antes de las cinco y media.**
  *One must (You should) return before 5:30.*

**B.** Circle the most appropriate impersonal expression from the parentheses to complete the sentences below. The first one is done for you.

1. ( **Hay que** / **Es divertido** ) montar a caballo en la playa.

2. ( **Es interesante** / **Es necesario** ) hacer planes antes de salir de vacaciones.

3. ( **Es malo** / **Es interesante** ) visitar el zoológico.

4. ( **Hay que** / **Es divertido** ) hacer las reservaciones del hotel un mes antes de salir.

5. ( **Es necesario** / **Es malo** ) descansar mucho durante las vacaciones.

**C.** Using the words given as clues, write full sentences. Remember to use the infinitive after the verbs expressing plans, desires, wishes, and obligations.

Modelo   Ramiro / querer / viajar al campo

    *Ramiro quiere viajar al campo* _____.

1. Jorge y Sara / necesitar / regresar a casa

_____.

2. A Marieli / le / encantar / bucear

_____.

3. Hay que / calentar el caldo

_____.

4. Luz y yo / pensar / pasear en bote

_____.

5. Yo / tener que / pasar tiempo con mis tíos

_____.

6. Es divertido / hacer una fogata

_____.

7. Tú y Bruni / desear / montar en bicicleta

_____.

Write the Spanish vocabulary word or phrase below each picture. Be sure to include the article for each noun.

_____

_____

_____

_____

_____

_____

_____

_____

_____

_____

_____

_____

_____

_____

_____

_____

_____

_____

## Capítulo 8A

Fecha _____

**Vocabulary Flash Cards, Sheet 2**

Write the Spanish vocabulary word or phrase below each picture. Be sure to include the article for each noun.

_____

_____

_____

_____

_____

_____

_____

_____

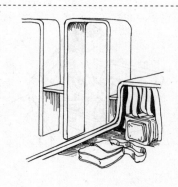

_____

_____

_____

_____

_____

_____

_____

_____

_____

_____

Write the Spanish vocabulary word below each picture. If there is a word or phrase, copy it in the space provided. Be sure to include the article for each noun.

abierto,
abierta

**Capítulo 8A**    Fecha _____    **Vocabulary Flash Cards, Sheet 4**

Copy the word or phrase in the space provided. Be sure to include the article for each noun.

| | | |
|---|---|---|
| **cerrado, cerrada**<br><br><br>_____ ,<br>_____ | **extranjero, extranjera**<br><br><br>_____ ,<br>_____ | **hacer un viaje**<br><br><br>_____<br>_____ _____ |
| **planear**<br><br><br><br>_____ | **la reservación**<br><br><br>_____<br>_____ | **abordar**<br><br><br><br>_____ |
| **con destino a**<br><br><br>_____<br>_____ _____ | **de ida y vuelta**<br><br><br>_____<br>_____ _____ | **directo, directa**<br><br><br>_____ ,<br>_____ |

Copy the word or phrase in the space provided. Be sure to include the article for each noun.

| | | |
|---|---|---|
| **durar** | **hacer escala** | **la línea aérea** |
| _____ | _____ _____ | _____ _____ |
| **la llegada** | **el retraso** | **la salida** |
| _____ _____ | _____ _____ | _____ _____ |
| **bienvenido, bienvenida** | **insistir en** | **listo, lista** |
| _____, _____ | _____ _____ | _____, _____ |

Copy the word or phrase in the space provided. Be sure to include the article for each noun. The blank cards can be used to write and practice other Spanish vocabulary in the chapter.

| | | |
|---|---|---|
| **sugerir** <br><br> _____ | **tendremos** <br><br> _____ | **tener paciencia** <br><br> _____ |
| **la aduana** <br><br> _____ <br> _____ | **el empleado, la empleada** <br><br> _____ _____, <br> _____ _____ | **facturar** <br><br> _____ |
| <br><br> _____ | <br><br> _____ | <br><br> _____ |

Tear out this page. Write the English words on the lines. Fold the paper along the dotted line to see the correct answers so you can check your work.

la agencia de viajes _____

el equipaje _____

extranjero, extranjera _____

hacer un viaje _____

la maleta _____

planear _____

abordar _____

la aduana _____

el aeropuerto _____

el anuncio _____

de ida y vuelta _____

la salida _____

el vuelo _____

abierto, abierta _____

Fold In ←

Tear out this page. Write the Spanish words on the lines. Fold the paper along the
dotted line to see the correct answers so you can check your work.

travel agency        _____

luggage              _____

foreign              _____


to take a trip       _____

suitcase             _____

to plan              _____

to board             _____

customs              _____

airport              _____

announcement         _____

round-trip           _____

departure            _____

flight               _____

open                 _____

Fold In ←

Tear out this page. Write the English words on the lines. Fold the paper along the dotted line to see the correct answers so you can check your work.

el pasaporte          _____

la reservación        _____

el turista,           _____
la turista

directo, directa      _____

durar                 _____

el empleado,          _____
la empleada

la línea aérea        _____

el pasajero,          _____
la pasajera

registrar             _____


bienvenido,           _____
bienvenida

necesitar             _____

permitir              _____

preferir              _____

cerrado, cerrada      _____

Fold In

Nombre _____     Hora _____

**Capítulo 8A**     Fecha _____     **Vocabulary Check, Sheet 4**

Tear out this page. Write the Spanish words on the lines. Fold the paper along the dotted line to see the correct answers so you can check your work.

passport                    _____

reservation                 _____

tourist                     _____

direct                      _____

to last                     _____

employee                    _____

airline                     _____

passenger                   _____

to inspect, to              _____
search (*luggage*)

welcome                     _____

to need                     _____

to allow, to permit         _____

to prefer                   _____

closed                      _____

Fold In ←

# The present subjunctive (p. 410)

- You form the present subjunctive in the same way that you form negative **tú** commands and **usted/ustedes** commands. You drop the **-o** of the present-tense indicative **yo** form and add the present subjunctive endings. See the chart below:

| hablar | | aprender | | escribir | |
|---|---|---|---|---|---|
| hable | hable**mos** | aprend**a** | aprend**amos** | escrib**a** | escrib**amos** |
| hable**s** | habl**éis** | aprend**as** | aprend**áis** | escrib**as** | escrib**áis** |
| hable | habl**en** | aprend**a** | aprend**an** | escrib**a** | escrib**an** |

**A.** Write the subjunctive ending for each of the verbs below. Follow the model.

**Modelo**   yo / asistir          asist _a_____

1. los pasajeros / abordar          abord_____

2. tú / beber          beb_____

3. nosotros / viajar          viaj_____

4. el vuelo / durar          dur_____

5. tú / desear          dese_____

6. yo / vivir          viv_____

7. la familia / planear          plane_____

8. nosotros / llevar          llev_____

- The present subjunctive has the same spelling changes that you used with the negative **tú** commands and **usted/ustedes** commands.
- Here are the present subjunctive forms of **llegar** and **sacar**:

| llegar | | sacar | |
|---|---|---|---|
| lle**gue** | lle**guemos** | sa**que** | sa**quemos** |
| lle**gues** | lle**guéis** | sa**ques** | sa**quéis** |
| lle**gue** | lle**guen** | sa**que** | sa**quen** |

# The present subjunctive (*continued*)

**B.** Look at the sentences using the present subjunctive below. Underline the second verb in each and then circle the spelling change in each verb that you underlined. The first one has been done for you.

1.  La profesora recomienda que nosotros <u>sa(qu)emos</u> más libros de la biblioteca.

2.  Yo necesito que ustedes paguen por los boletos hoy.

3.  Se recomienda que los empleados busquen cosas prohibidas.

4.  El niño desea que la mamá no apague la luz.

5.  Prefiero que tú llegues a tiempo.

6.  El entrenador quiere que los jugadores jueguen todos los días de esta semana.

7.  El Sr. Vega prohíbe que nosotros toquemos las exposiciones.

8.  Papá recomienda que yo me seque las manos.

• The same verbs that have irregular **yo** forms in the present indicative are also irregular in the present subjunctive.

• Here are the conjugations of two verbs that have this irregular pattern:

| tener | | conocer | |
|---|---|---|---|
| tenga | tengamos | conozca | conozcamos |
| tengas | tengáis | conozcas | conozcáis |
| tenga | tengan | conozca | conozcan |

**C.** Write the irregular **yo** form of the present indicative for the first part of each example below. Then, write the correct present subjunctive form using the cues given in the second part. The first one is done for you.

| | Present Indicative | | Present Subjunctive | |
|---|---|---|---|---|
| 1. traer | yo | *traigo* | Andrés y Toni | *traigan* |
| 2. decir | yo | _____ | tú | _____ |
| 3. conducir | yo | _____ | Diego | _____ |
| 4. salir | yo | _____ | yo | _____ |
| 5. ofrecer | yo | _____ | Ana y Javier | _____ |
| 6. venir | yo | _____ | tú | _____ |
| 7. hacer | yo | _____ | María y yo | _____ |
| 8. oír | yo | _____ | Ud. | _____ |

**Capítulo 8A**

# The present subjunctive (*continued*)

**D.** Write the correct present subjunctive forms of the verbs given. The first one is done for you.

**El agente de viajes sugiere que...**

1. ...nosotros ____*hablemos*____ (**hablar**) con el piloto antes de salir.

2. ...yo _____ (**buscar**) un asiento cerca de la ventanilla.

3. ...mis padres _____ (**llegar**) temprano al aeropuerto.

4. ...nosotros _____ (**hacer**) las reservaciones con el hotel.

5. ...tú _____ (**traer**) el bloqueador solar.

6. ...yo no _____ (**salir**) sin mi pasaporte.

7. ...mis hermanos y yo _____ (**obedecer**) las reglas del viajero.

8. ...Pedro _____ (**pasar**) a la salida.

• The present subjunctive is used when one person is influencing the actions of another, by advising, prohibiting, or suggesting. Some verbs that often introduce the subjunctive mood are:

| | | | | | |
|---|---|---|---|---|---|
| **decir** | *to say; to tell* | **preferir** | *to prefer* | **querer** | *to want* |
| **insistir en** | *to insist upon* | **permitir** | *to permit* | **prohibir** | *to prohibit* |
| **necesitar** | *to need* | **recomendar** | *to recommend* | **sugerir** | *to suggest* |

• These verbs are used in the indicative, but the verbs that follow them are used in the subjunctive. The word **que** connects the two parts of the sentence.

**Indicative**        **Subjunctive**

Su madre le <u>prohibe</u> *que* Agustina <u>salga</u> de la casa después de las nueve.

El profesor <u>recomienda</u> *que* nosotros <u>visitemos</u> el zoológico.

# The present subjunctive (*continued*)

- Subjunctive sentences have two parts, each part with its own subject. Notice that the first part uses the present indicative to recommend, suggest, prohibit, and so on:

  **El agente de viajes quiere...**

- The second part uses the present subjunctive to say what the other subject should or should not do:

  **...nosotros visitemos el zoológico.**

  **El agente de viajes quiere que nosotros visitemos el zoológico.**
  *The travel agent wants us to visit the zoo.*

**E.** Read the following sentences. In each sentence, underline the verb that shows that one person is trying to influence the action of another (present indicative) and circle the verb that indicates what the other person should do (present subjunctive). Follow the model.

Modelo   Mi maestro <u>permite</u> que nosotros ⟨trabajemos⟩ en grupos.

1. La agente de viajes sugiere que ellos visiten La Paz.

2. El aduanero insiste en que tú tengas el pasaporte en la mano.

3. Los hermanos necesitan que los padres aborden con ellos.

4. El piloto les dice a los pasajeros que apaguen los teléfonos celulares.

5. El tío recomienda que nosotros facturemos el equipaje temprano.

**F.** In each sentence below, underline the verb that shows that one person is trying to influence the action of another. Then, write the subjunctive form of the verb in parentheses. Follow the model.

Modelo   Carlos <u>sugiere</u> que nosotros ___*pasemos*___ a la casa de cambios. (**pasar**)

1. Pancho sugiere que Julián y Lolis _____ los pasaportes a la aduana. (**traer**)

2. Los auxiliares de vuelo recomiendan que yo _____ jugo de manzana. (**beber**)

3. Yo quiero que los auxiliares de vuelo me _____. (**ayudar**)

4. La profesora le dice a Sofía que ella _____ sobre los lugares que visita. (**aprender**)

5. La aduanera permite que tú _____ la maleta ahora. (**hacer**)

# The present subjunctive (*continued*)

**G.** Fill in the blank in the first part of each sentence below with the present indicative form of the verb to show that someone wants to influence another person's actions. In the second part of the sentence, fill in the blanks with the subjunctive form of the verb to say what someone should do. The first one is done for you.

1. Óscar (**sugerir**) _____*sugiere*_____ que nosotros (**visitar**) _____*visitemos*_____ la casa de cambio antes de salir.

2. Nosotros (**recomendar**) _____ que Uds. (**comprar**) _____ una guía de la ciudad.

3. La empleada (**necesitar**) _____ que tú le _____ (**escribir**) tu número de pasaporte.

4. Esa agente de vuelos (**prohibir**) _____ que los pasajeros (**llegar**) _____ tarde.

5. Mis padres (**preferir**) _____ que yo (**comer**) _____ con ellos.

6. Los auxiliares de vuelo (**insistir**) _____ en que nosotros (**obedecer**) _____ a los señales (*signs*).

**H.** Use the words given to write complete sentences in the order in which the words appear. Follow the model.

*Remember:* The verb that shows that one person is trying to influence the action of another uses the present indicative while the verb that tells what the other person should do uses the present subjunctive.

**Modelo**   Felipe / insistir en / que / Amelia / tener paciencia
   *Felipe insiste en que Amelia tenga paciencia* _____ .

1. Los profesores / sugerir / que / los estudiantes / estudiar más horas

   _____ .

2. Nosotros / recomendar / que / Uds. / llegar temprano a los exámenes

   _____ .

3. Mis padres / querer / que / yo / asistir a una buena universidad

   _____ .

4. Mamá / necesitar / que / nosotros / poner la mesa

   _____ .

5. Yo / preferir / que / tú / buscar otro trabajo

   _____ .

# Irregular verbs in the subjunctive (p. 413)

- Verbs with irregular **tú** and **usted/ustedes** commands also have irregular subjunctive forms.

| dar | | estar | | ir | | saber | | ser | |
|-----|-----|-------|---------|-------|---------|-------|---------|------|---------|
| dé | demos | esté | estemos | vaya | vayamos | sepa | sepamos | sea | seamos |
| des | deis | estés | estéis | vayas | vayáis | sepas | sepáis | seas | seáis |
| dé | den | esté | estén | vaya | vayan | sepa | sepan | sea | sean |

**A.** Read each sentence below and circle the verb in its subjunctive form. Then, write the infinitive of the circled verb in the blank. Follow the model.

**Modelo**   Recomiendo que Ana te (dé)la tarjeta de embarque. _____*dar*_____

1. Sugiero que el pasajero esté aquí a las cuatro. _____

2. Quiero que vayas a la agencia de viajes. _____

3. Deseo que sepas la hora de llegada. _____

4. Insisto en que sean responsables. _____

5. Necesito que el vuelo sea de ida y vuelta. _____

**B.** Circle the second subject in each sentence. Then, write the correct form of the verb in parentheses using the present subjunctive. The first one is done for you.

1. Deseo que (ustedes) ____*estén*____ en el aeropuerto muy temprano. (**estar**)

2. Recomiendo que ustedes _____ sus maletas a los empleados. (**dar**)

3. Sugiero que tú _____ a la agencia de viajes. (**ir**)

4. Quiero que ella _____ dónde está la puerta de embarque. (**saber**)

5. Necesito que la maleta _____ grande. (**ser**)

6. La empleada de la aerolínea quiere que yo le _____ mi tarjeta de embarque. (**dar**)

**Capítulo 8A**

Fecha _____

# Lectura: Ecuador, país de maravillas (pp. 418–419)

**A.** The reading in your textbook is about the South American country of Ecuador. Write three things that you would expect to find in your reading about its tourist attractions.

1. _____ .

2. _____ .

3. _____ .

**B.** You can often predict what a reading is about by looking at the title, subheads, and photo captions. Look at the photos and read the captions on pages 418–419 of your textbook. Place an *X* next to the attractions you can find in Ecuador.

| Las atracciones turísticas del Ecuador | |
|---|---|
| _____ woven cloth | _____ la Mitad del Mundo |
| _____ the island of Puerto Rico | _____ snow-covered mountains |
| _____ the Galapagos Islands | _____ the church of La Compañía de Jesús |

**C.** Read the excerpt from your reading and circle the letter of the answers to the questions that follow.

║ *Es un país pequeño, pero tiene paisajes para todos los gustos (tastes): desde playas tropicales hasta montañas nevadas, desde ciudades coloniales hasta parques naturales. Ecuador es una joya.* ║

1. ¿Qué clase de país es Ecuador?
   a. Es un país pequeño.
   b. Es un país grande.

2. ¿Dónde nieva en Ecuador?
   a. Nieva en las playas tropicales.
   b. Nieva en las montañas.

3. ¿Hay ciudades coloniales en Ecuador?
   a. Sí, hay ciudades coloniales en Ecuador.
   b. No, no hay ciudades coloniales en Ecuador.

4. ¿Qué clase de parques hay en Ecuador?
   a. Hay parques artificiales en Ecuador.
   b. Hay parques naturales en Ecuador.

# Presentación oral (p. 421)

**Task:** Imagine that you work at a travel agency. You need to provide travel information to a client who would like to travel to a Spanish-speaking country.

**A.** Choose one of the following Spanish-speaking countries: Mexico or Ecuador.

**B.** Read the following travel information about each country. Then, circle one or two recommendations you would offer based on what you read.

1. La ciudad de Quito en Ecuador está en las montañas y hace mucho frío. Hay una iglesia muy importante.
   **a.** Recomiendo que lleven poca ropa.
   **b.** Sugiero que vayan a la iglesia La Compañía de Jesús.
   **c.** Recomiendo que lleven suéteres o chaquetas.

2. Cancún está en México. En Cancún hay una playa tropical de 14 millas y muchos hoteles elegantes.
   **a.** Si desean ir a una playa grande, yo recomiendo que vayan a Cancún.
   **b.** Si buscan un hotel elegante, vayan a Cancún.
   **c.** Recomiendo que lleven trajes de baño.

**C.** Use your recommendations in **part B** as a model for your oral presentation. You may use the sentence starters below. Don't forget to use the subjunctive when you are advising, prohibiting, or suggesting something to your client.

*Recomiendo que Uds. viajen a* _____ . *Allí pueden ver*

_____ . *Deben llevar* _____

*porque* _____ .

**D.** Now, practice your presentation using the information you have gathered. Try to present the information in a logical sequence and speak clearly.

**E.** Present the trip you have planned to your partner. Your teacher will grade you on the following:

- how much information you communicate
- how easy it is to understand you

Nombre _____    Hora _____

**Capítulo 8B**    Fecha _____    **Vocabulary Flash Cards, Sheet 1**

Write the Spanish vocabulary word or phrase below each picture. Be sure to include the article for each noun.

_____

_____

_____

_____

_____

_____

_____

_____

_____

_____

_____

_____

_____

_____

_____

_____

_____

_____

Write the Spanish vocabulary word or phrase below each picture. Be sure to include the article for each noun.

_____

_____

_____

_____

_____

_____

_____

_____

_____

_____

_____

_____

_____

_____

_____

**Capítulo 8B**     Fecha _____     **Vocabulary Flash Cards, Sheet 3**

Write the Spanish vocabulary word or phrase below each picture. Be sure to include the article for each noun.

_____

_____

_____

_____

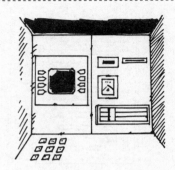

_____

_____

_____

_____

_____

_____

_____

_____

_____

_____

_____

_____

_____

_____

Nombre _____  Hora _____

**Capítulo 8B**

Fecha _____  **Vocabulary Flash Cards, Sheet 4**

Write the Spanish vocabulary word below each picture. If there is a word or phrase, copy it in the space provided. Be sure to include the article for each noun.

| | | |
|---|---|---|
| _____ | _____ | _____ |
| **histórico, histórica** | **atento, atenta** | **ofender** |
| _____, _____ | _____, | _____ |
| **puntual** | **disfrutar de** | **la excursión** |
| _____ | _____ | _____ |
| | _____ | |

Copy the word or phrase in the space provided.

| | | |
|---|---|---|
| **regatear** | **bello, bella** | **en punto** |
| _____ | _____, _____ | _____ |
| **estupendo, estupenda** | **famoso, famosa** | **siguiente** |
| _____, _____ | _____, _____ | _____ |
| **tal vez** | **típico, típica** | **hacer ruido** |
| _____ _____ | _____, _____ | _____ |

Copy the word or phrase in the space provided. Be sure to include the article for each noun. The blank cards can be used to write and practice other Spanish vocabulary in the chapter.

| | | |
|---|---|---|
| **conseguir**<br><br>_____ | **observar**<br><br>_____ | _____ |
| _____ | _____ | _____ |
| _____ | _____ | _____ |

Tear out this page. Write the English words on the lines. Fold the paper along the dotted line to see the correct answers so you can check your work.

la casa de cambio _____

el palacio _____

el quiosco _____

el ascensor _____

la llave _____

la recepción _____

la artesanía _____

el bote de vela _____

el guía, la guía _____

bello, bella _____

en punto _____

famoso, famosa _____

siguiente _____

tal vez _____

Fold In →

Tear out this page. Write the Spanish words on the lines. Fold the paper along the dotted line to see the correct answers so you can check your work.

currency exchange  _____

palace  _____

newsstand  _____

elevator  _____

key  _____

reception desk  _____

handicrafts  _____

sailboat  _____

guide  _____

beautiful  _____

exactly (time)  _____

famous  _____

next, following  _____

maybe, perhaps  _____

Fold In ←

Tear out this page. Write the English words on the lines. Fold the paper along the dotted line to see the correct answers so you can check your work.

el cajero automático _____

la catedral _____

histórico, histórica _____

conseguir _____

la habitación _____

cortés _____

hacer ruido _____

ofender _____

la propina _____

cambiar _____

disfrutar de _____

navegar _____

el vendedor, _____
la vendedora

típico, típica _____

Fold In

Tear out this page. Write the Spanish words on the lines. Fold the paper along the dotted line to see the correct answers so you can check your work.

ATM _____

cathedral _____

historical _____

to obtain _____

room _____

polite _____

to make noise _____

to offend _____

tip _____

to change,
to exchange _____

to enjoy _____

to sail, to navigate _____

vendor _____

typical _____

Fold In ←

# Present subjunctive with impersonal expressions (p. 436)

- You can use impersonal expressions, such as **es importante, es necesario, es mejor,** and **es bueno,** to tell people what they should do. Sentences with these impersonal expressions are often followed by **que** + subjunctive:

    **Es necesario que nosotros le demos una propina al empleado.**
    *It's necessary that we give a tip to the employee.*

    **Es mejor que tú observes las reglas para el viaje.**
    *It's better that you observe the rules for the trip.*

**A.** Choose the correct verb form in parentheses to complete each sentence. Follow the model.

**Modelo** Es importante que nosotros ( (llevemos) / llevamos ) la llave.

1. Es mejor que nosotros ( visitamos / visitemos ) la catedral.

2. Es necesario que ustedes ( van / vayan ) a la recepción.

3. Es bueno que tú ( tomas / tomes ) el ascensor.

4. Es importante que yo ( cambie / cambia ) dinero.

5. Es mejor que el grupo ( haga / hace ) una gira de la capital.

**B.** Read the sentences below. Fill in the blanks with the correct form of the verbs in parentheses. The first one is done for you.

1. Es importante que ustedes _____*visiten*_____ el castillo. (**visitar**)

2. Es necesario que tú _____ la guía. (**llevar**)

3. Es bueno que nosotros _____ en un bote de vela. (**navegar**)

4. Es mejor que yo _____ una gira. (**hacer**)

5. Es importante que Mateo _____ los lugares históricos. (**conocer**)

6. Es necesario que usted _____ dinero en la casa de cambio. (**cambiar**)

7. Es mejor que nosotros _____ un lugar para comer ahora. (**buscar**)

8. Es bueno que Ignacio y Javier _____ con nosotros. (**ir**)

# Present subjunctive with impersonal expressions (*continued*)

- To speak generally about things that should or should not be done, use an impersonal expression plus an infinitive. Note that **que** is not used. Compare the following sentences:

**Subjunctive**
**Es importante que tú** *seas* **cortés.** *It is important that you be polite.* (specific)

**Infinitive**
**Es importante** *ser* **cortés.** *It is important to be polite.* (general)

**C.** Read the following sentences. Write **S** (for specific) if the sentence mentions specific people. Write **G** (for general) if it does not mention specific people. Follow the models.

**Modelo 1** ___G___ Es necesario ser puntual.

**Modelo 2** ___S___ Es necesario que ustedes sean puntuales.

1. _____ Es necesario estar atento en el bote de vela.

2. _____ No es bueno que nosotros hagamos ruido en las habitaciones.

3. _____ Es importante que tú observes al guía.

4. _____ Es mejor no ofender a los reyes.

5. _____ Es bueno dar propinas.

6. _____ Es importante que usted sea cortés con los vendedores.

**D.** Read each sentence and decide if it needs the subjunctive (*specific*) or the infinitive (*general*). Then, fill in the blank with the correct form of the verb given. Follow the models.

**Modelo 1** Es esencial _____*dar*_____ (**dar**) propinas.

**Modelo 2** Es necesario que la abuela _____*suba*_____ (**subir**) en el ascensor.

1. Es necesario _____ (**cambiar**) dinero en el banco.

2. Es importante _____ (**llevar**) las llaves del hotel.

3. Es bueno que tú _____ (**sacar**) muchas fotos en la ciudad.

4. Es mejor _____ (**llegar**) temprano al aeropuerto.

5. Es importante que nosotros _____ (**ser**) corteses.

# Present subjunctive of stem-changing verbs (p. 439)

- Stem-changing verbs ending in **-ar** and **-er** have the same stem changes in the subjunctive as in the indicative. Just like the present indicative, the **nosotros** and **vosotros** forms do not have a stem change.
- Here are the conjugations for **cerrar** and **volver:**

| cerrar (e → ie) | | volver (o → ue) | |
|---|---|---|---|
| cierre | cerremos | vuelva | volvamos |
| cierres | cerréis | vuelvas | volváis |
| cierre | cierren | vuelva | vuelvan |

**A.** Read each sentence and complete the verb with the correct stem-changing vowels. Follow the model.

**Modelo**   (**recordar**)  Es necesario que usted rec _ue_ rde la dirección.

1. (**encender**)  Es importante que tú enc_____ndas las luces antes de entrar.

2. (**empezar**)  La profesora quiere que Simón emp_____ce con el examen ahora.

3. (**contar**)  Es mejor que tú c_____ntes el dinero fuera de la tienda.

4. (**poder**)  Es bueno que ustedes p_____dan visitar tantos lugares.

5. (**llover**)  Hace mal tiempo, pero es mejor que no ll_____va durante el partido de béisbol.

**B.** Complete the following sentences with the subjunctive form of the verb in parentheses. The first one is done for you.

1. Es mejor que nosotros _almorcemos_ bien antes de ir de excursión. (**almorzar**)

2. Es importante que tú _____ lo que el guía dice. (**entender**)

3. Rosa no tiene dinero. Es necesario que ella _____ un cajero automático. (**encontrar**)

4. Es bueno que ustedes se _____ temprano para visitar el castillo. (**despertar**)

5. Marta no conoce la ciudad. Es mejor que yo le _____ un buen hotel. (**recomendar**)

6. Antes de salir del hotel, es importante que ellos _____ la llave. (**devolver**)

7. El camarero sugiere que nosotros _____ la cena ahora. (**comenzar**)

# Present subjunctive of stem-changing verbs (*continued*)

- Stem-changing verbs ending in **-ir** have changes in all forms of the present subjunctive.
- Here are the conjugations for **pedir, dormir,** and **divertirse:**

| **pedir** (e → i) | | **dormir** (o → ue), (o → u) | | **divertirse** (e → ie), (e → i) | |
|---|---|---|---|---|---|
| pida | pidamos | duerma | durmamos | me divierta | nos divirtamos |
| pidas | pidáis | duermas | durmáis | te diviertas | os divirtáis |
| pida | pidan | duerma | duerman | se divierta | se diviertan |

**C.** Complete the following sentences using the present subjunctive of the **-ir** stem-changing verbs in parentheses. Follow the model.

**Modelo**   (pedir) Es necesario que ustedes _____*pidan*_____ ayuda.

1. (**repetir**) Los turistas quieren que la guía _____ la explicación.

2. (**sentirse**) Deseamos que nuestros parientes _____ bien.

3. (**divertirse**) Nuestros padres quieren que nosotros _____ mucho.

4. (**seguir**) Es importante que nosotros _____ las instrucciones.

5. (**dormir**) Es mejor que Felipe y Ana _____ en el avión.

**D.** Use the words given to write complete sentences in the order in which the words appear. Follow the model.

**Modelo**   Es bueno / que / ustedes / divertirse / en las vacaciones
  _Es bueno que ustedes se diviertan en las vacaciones_____.

1. Es necesario / que / tú / conseguir / una llave para la habitación

   _____.

2. Yo no / querer / que / mi hermano / reírse / de mí

   _____.

3. Es importante / que / yo / hervir / los huevos primero

   _____.

4. Es mejor / que / el camarero / servir / la comida ahora

   _____.

5. El jefe / recomendar / que / nosotros / pedir / una propina

   _____.

**Capítulo 8B**

## Lectura: Antigua, una ciudad colonial (pp. 444–445)

**A.** The reading in your textbook is a travel brochure about Antigua, Guatemala. Look at the photos, the heads, and the subheads in this brochure to get an idea of what the reading will be about. What are three things this brochure might mention?

1. _____, 2. _____, 3. _____

**B.** Read the following excerpt from the reading in your textbook and complete the sentences below.

> *¿Qué hay que ver en la ciudad de Antigua?*
>
> *La ciudad de Antigua tiene muchos sitios de interés. Se puede apreciar toda la historia de esta ciudad mirando sus casas y monumentos coloniales. En el centro de la ciudad está la Plaza Mayor. Los edificios principales son el Ayuntamiento (City Hall), la Catedral y el Palacio de los Capitanes.*

1. In the city of Antigua, you can see _____.
   **a.** interesting places        **b.** hotels

2. The Plaza Mayor is in _____.
   **a.** the center of the city        **b.** Tikal

3. The Palacio de los Capitanes is _____.
   **a.** a sailboat        **b.** one of the important buildings

**C.** The name **Antigua** means *antique*, or *old* in Spanish. Read this introduction from the reading. Then, write some of the words or phrases that indicate the city is old. One example is provided for you.

> *Situada a 45 minutos de la Ciudad de Guatemala, Antigua le fascina al turista por sus calles de piedras, su arquitectura colonial y sus ruinas de iglesias y monasterios. El español Francisco de la Cueva fundó la ciudad el 10 de marzo de 1543. La "Ciudad de las Perpetuas Rosas," nombrada así por sus jardines con flores, tiene un clima muy agradable y preserva un sabor colonial único. Caminar por sus calles es como visitar el pasado y descubrir una ciudad típica española del siglo (century) XVII.*

calle de piedras _____

_____

_____

# Presentación escrita (p. 447)

**Task:** Imagine you are going to visit a Spanish-speaking country with a group. Prepare an illustrated brochure so you can share your experience with others.

**A.** Think about the preparations you must make before you go on your trip. Answer the questions below to help you organize your brochure.

1. ¿Qué país vas a visitar? _____

2. ¿Cómo vas a viajar? _____

3. ¿Qué vas a llevar? _____

4. ¿Qué lugares vas a visitar? _____

   _____

5. ¿Qué actividades vas a hacer? _____

   _____

**B.** Use the information from **part A** to complete the sentences below. You can use the following paragraph as a model.

> *Voy a viajar a México. Voy a viajar por avión. Es importante que yo lleve una guía porque voy a visitar el centro histórico y el famoso castillo. También es bueno que yo haga excursiones y navegue en el océano.*

Voy a viajar a _____. Voy a viajar por _____. Es importante

que yo lleve _____ porque voy a visitar _____ y

_____. También es bueno que yo _____ y

_____.

**C.** Choose some illustrations for your brochure. You can use photos from home or from magazines, or you can draw pictures to illustrate what you will see and do on your trip.

**D.** Reread your draft and check the spelling, vocabulary, and verb usage. Share your draft with a classmate, who will check for clarity, organization, and errors.

**E.** Make a new version of the brochure with changes and corrections. Don't forget to attach your illustrations for the brochure where they will be most appropriate.

# A ver si recuerdas: Verbs with spelling changes in the present tense (p. 453)

- As you know, some verbs have spelling changes in the present tense for reasons of pronunciation. Some verbs, such as **escoger, recoger, seguir,** and **conseguir,** change spelling only in the *yo* form.

  **Mi hermano *escoge* unas vacaciones en las montañas mientras que yo *escojo* la playa.**
  *My brother chooses a vacation in the mountains while I choose the beach.*

  **Los turistas no siempre *siguen* las reglas; yo sí las *sigo*.**
  *The tourists do not always follow the rules; I do follow them.*

- Other verbs, such as **enviar** and **esquiar,** simply add accent marks on the **i** in all persons except **nosotros** and **vosotros.**

  **Mi hermano *esquía* mucho. Nosotros *esquiamos* juntos a veces.**
  *My brother skis a lot. We ski together sometimes.*

**A.** Write the present tense **yo** form of the infinitives below. Then write the second form in the present tense using the cue provided. Follow the model.

| Modelo | escoger | yo _*escojo*_ | usted _*escoge*_ |
|---|---|---|---|
| 1. | conseguir | yo _____ | tú _____ |
| 2. | enviar | yo _____ | nosotros _____ |
| 3. | recoger | yo _____ | ellas _____ |
| 4. | seguir | yo _____ | ella _____ |
| 5. | escoger | yo _____ | nosotras _____ |
| 6. | esquiar | yo _____ | tú _____ |

## A ver si recuerdas: Verbs with spelling changes in the present tense (*continued*)

**B.** Pablo is working at a summer camp. Complete his letter home by writing the **yo** form of the verbs given. The first one is done for you.

*Queridos padres:*

*¿Cómo están? Yo estoy muy bien aquí en las montañas, y estoy trabajando*

*mucho. Todos los días yo _____sigo_____ (**seguir**) las instrucciones de*

*mi jefe. Siempre _____ (**recoger**) la basura de la cafetería y*

*_____ (**enviar**) las cartas de los niños. Después, yo _____*

*(**conseguir**) el horario del día del director del campamento. Lo*

*_____ (**seguir**) con cuidado, y por la tarde tengo dos horas libres.*

*A veces _____ (**esquiar**) en agua—¡mi actividad favorita! Por la noche,*

*yo _____ (**escoger**) un juego para jugar con los niños. Siempre me*

*acuesto muy cansado.*

*Un abrazo,*

*Pablo*

**C.** Complete the following answers, paying special attention to the verbs with spelling changes. Follow the model.

**Modelo**    ¿Les envías muchas cartas a tus parientes?

Sí, yo siempre les _____*envío cartas*_____.

**1.** ¿Quién recoge la basura en tu casa?

Yo _____ en mi casa.

**2.** ¿Esquías todos los inviernos?

Sí, yo _____.

**3.** ¿Siempre sigues las reglas de tus padres?

Sí, yo siempre _____.

**4.** ¿Dónde consigues regalos para tus parientes?

Yo _____.

Write the Spanish vocabulary word below each picture. Be sure to include the article for each noun.

_____

_____

_____

_____

_____

_____

_____

_____

_____

**Capítulo 9A**

Write the Spanish vocabulary word below each picture. Be sure to include the article for each noun.

_____

_____

_____

_____

_____

_____

_____

_____

_____

_____

_____

_____

_____

_____

_____

_____

_____

_____

Write the Spanish vocabulary word below each picture. Be sure to include the article for each noun.

Write the Spanish vocabulary word below each picture. Be sure to include the article for each noun.

_____

_____

_____

_____

_____

_____

_____

_____

_____

_____

_____

_____

_____

_____

_____

_____

_____

_____

Write the Spanish vocabulary word below each picture. If there is a word or phrase, copy it in the space provided. Be sure to include the article for each noun.

_____

_____

_____

_____

_____

_____

_____

_____

_____

_____

**la
ley**

_____

_____

**la
política**

_____

_____

**algún
día**

_____

_____

**los
beneficios**

_____

_____

Copy the word or phrase in the space provided. Be sure to include the article for each noun.

| | | |
|---|---|---|
| **bilingüe**<br><br><br><br>_____ | **la carrera**<br><br><br><br>_____ | **la escuela técnica**<br><br><br><br>_____ _____ |
| **el futuro**<br><br><br>____<br>_____ | **ganarse la vida**<br><br><br><br>_____ _____ | **habrá**<br><br><br><br>_____ |
| **el idioma**<br><br><br>____<br>_____ | **militar**<br><br><br><br>_____ | **el programa de estudios**<br><br><br>_____ _____<br>_____ _____ |

Copy the word or phrase in the space provided. Be sure to include the article for each noun. The blank cards can be used to write and practice other Spanish vocabulary for the chapter.

| | | |
|---|---|---|
| **el salario** | **seguir (una carrera)** | **el dueño, la dueña** |
| _____ _____ | _____ _____ | _____ _____, _____ _____ |
| **el gerente, la gerente** | **las artes** | **el derecho** |
| _____ _____, _____ _____ | _____ _____ | _____ _____ |
| **la profesión** | | |
| _____ _____ | _____ _____ | _____ _____ |

These blank cards can be used to write and practice other Spanish vocabulary for the chapter.

|  |  |  |
|---|---|---|
| _____ | _____ | _____ |
| _____ | _____ | _____ |
| _____ | _____ | _____ |

**Capítulo 9A**

Tear out this page. Write the English words on the lines. Fold the paper along the dotted line to see the correct answers so you can check your work.

el científico,
la científica          _____

el ingeniero,
la ingeniera          _____

el veterinario,
la veterinaria          _____

el contador,
la contadora          _____

el dueño, la dueña          _____

el gerente,
la gerente          _____

los negocios          _____

el hombre de
negocios, la mujer
de negocios          _____

el secretario,
la secretaria          _____

el artista, la artista          _____

el abogado,
la abogada          _____

el derecho          _____

el colegio          _____

la universidad          _____

Fold In

**Capítulo 9A**

Fecha _____

Tear out this page. Write the Spanish words on the lines. Fold the paper along the dotted line to see the correct answers so you can check your work.

scientist _____

engineer _____

veterinarian _____

accountant _____

owner _____

manager _____

business _____

businessman, _____

businesswoman _____

secretary _____

artist _____

lawyer _____

(study of) law _____

high school _____

university _____

Fold In

Tear out this page. Write the English words on the lines. Fold the paper along the dotted line to see the correct answers so you can check your work.

el agricultor,
la agricultora          _____

el arquitecto,
la arquitecta           _____

el diseñador,
la diseñadora           _____

el mecánico,
la mecánica             _____

el cartero,
la cartera              _____

el escritor,
la escritora            _____

el pintor, la pintora   _____

la ley                  _____

la política             _____

el político,
la política             _____

bilingüe                _____

la carrera              _____

el salario              _____

la profesión            _____

Fold In →

Tear out this page. Write the Spanish words on the lines. Fold the paper along the dotted line to see the correct answers so you can check your work.

farmer        _____

architect     _____

designer      _____

mechanic      _____

mail carrier  _____

writer        _____

painter       _____

law           _____

politics      _____

politician    _____

bilingual     _____

career        _____

salary        _____

profession    _____

Fold In ←

# The future tense (p. 464)

- The future tense tells what will happen. To form the future tense of regular verbs ending in **-ar**, **-er**, and **-ir**, add these endings to the infinitive: **-é, -ás, -á, -emos, -éis, -án.**

  **En unos años *seré* un abogado.**

  *In a few years, I will be a lawyer.*

- Here are the future forms for **trabajar**, **ser**, and **vivir**:

| yo | trabajar**é**<br>ser**é**<br>vivir**é** | nosotros/nosotras | trabajar**emos**<br>ser**emos**<br>vivir**emos** |
|---|---|---|---|
| tú | trabajar**ás**<br>ser**ás**<br>vivir**ás** | vosotros/vosotras | trabajar**éis**<br>ser**éis**<br>vivir**éis** |
| usted/él/ella | trabajar**á**<br>ser**á**<br>vivir**á** | ustedes/ellos/ellas | trabajar**án**<br>ser**án**<br>vivir**án** |

**A.** Fill in the blanks with the correct future tense ending of each verb using the cues provided. Follow the model.

> **Modelo**　los estudiantes  conseguir *án*

1. yo viajar_____

2. nosotros vivir_____

3. Beto se graduar_____

4. tú ir_____

5. ustedes ser_____

6. Lisa pintar_____

7. yo trabajar_____

8. nosotros comer_____

**B.** Write the future tense of the verbs in parentheses. Follow the model.

> **Modelo**　(**trabajar**) Tú ____*trabajarás*____ como gerente en una tienda grande.

1. (**asistir**) Uds. _____ a la universidad del estado.

2. (**ser**) Yo _____ el mejor científico de esta región.

3. (**hablar**) Nosotros _____ con gente famosa.

4. (**esquiar**) Pablo _____ en las montañas altas del mundo.

5. (**graduarse**) Tú te _____ el año que viene.

# The future tense (*continued*)

**C.** Look at the underlined verbs in the sentences. Complete each sentence by using the future tense to tell what people will do, according to the picture. The first one is done for you.

**1.** _____ _____ Jaime y Victoria <u>son</u> abogados, pero algún día

_____*serán*_____ jueces.

**2.** Mario <u>trabaja</u> de cartero, pero el año que viene él

_____ de mecánico.

**3.** La familia Pérez <u>vive</u> en un apartamento, pero algún día

la familia _____ en una casa.

**4.** Generalmente Pilar y Mateo no <u>ven</u> videos, pero mañana

ellos _____ la tele.

**5.** Isabel <u>es</u> estudiante, pero algún día

ella _____ política.

**6.** Yo no <u>escribo</u> muchas cartas, pero más tarde le

_____ a mi primo.

**Capítulo 9A**

# The future tense: irregular verbs (p. 466)

- Some verb stems are irregular in the future tense: **hacer → har-; poder → podr-; saber → sabr-; tener → tendr-; haber → habr-.**
- Though the stems are irregular, the endings for these verbs are the same as regular future tense verbs. Look at the verb **hacer.**

| HACER | | | |
|---|---|---|---|
| yo | **haré** | nosotros/nosotras | **haremos** |
| tú | **harás** | vosotros/vosotras | **haréis** |
| usted/él/ella | **hará** | ustedes/ellos/ellas | **harán** |

**A.** Write the correct future tense ending of the verb in parentheses for each sentence. Follow the model.

**Modelo** (**hacer**) Yo har _é_ la tarea esta tarde.

1. (**poder**) Ricardo podr_____ contarnos unos chistes.

2. (**tener**) Mis primos tendr_____ muchas oportunidades en ese trabajo.

3. (**saber**) Nosotros sabr_____ la verdad después de unos minutos.

4. (**haber**) Habr_____ mucha gente en las tiendas.

**B.** Read what these people will do in the future. Write the irregular future tense stem to complete the verb in each sentence. Follow the model.

**Modelo** (**poder**) Mis primos no _podr_ án venir a la fiesta.

1. (**hacer**) Nosotros _____emos ejercicio este fin de semana.

2. (**poder**) Yo _____é ayudarte con la tarea.

3. (**Saber**) ¿ _____á Juan llegar a tu casa?

4. (**Haber**) _____á una graduación el fin de semana.

5. (**tener**) Tú _____ás tiempo el viernes por la tarde.

6. (**poder**) Ustedes _____án terminar con la tarea esta noche.

7. (**tener**) Nosotros _____emos que ir a la escuela temprano.

# The future tense: irregular verbs (*continued*)

**C.** Complete each sentence in the future tense with the correct form of the verb in parentheses. The first one is done for you.

1. (**poder**) Francisco _____*podrá*_____ usar la computadora.

2. (**saber**) Tú _____ de ciencias.

3. (**hacer**) La veterinaria le _____ un examen a mi perro.

4. (**poder**) Marta _____ ser contadora.

5. (**tener**) Mis amigos y yo _____ clases en la universidad.

6. (**haber**) En junio _____ una graduación.

**D.** Follow Isidro's list of things that he wants to do after graduation. Use the future tense of the verbs in parentheses. The first one is done for you.

**Después de graduarme...**

1. ...yo _____*podré*_____ hacer un viaje con mis amigos. (**poder**)

2. ...nosotros _____ a Europa. (**ir**)

3. ...mis amigos y yo _____ mucho dinero. (**gastar**)

4. ...mis padres no _____ qué hago cada minuto de cada día. (**saber**)

5. ...mi hermano _____ un trabajo, pero yo no. (**buscar**)

6. ...yo _____ a una universidad. (**asistir**)

7. ..._____ muchas oportunidades para mí. (**haber**)

## Lectura: ¡Descubre tu futuro! (pp. 472–473)

**A.** The reading in your textbook is about a career center. Read the heads and subheads to find out some basic information. Then, place an *X* next to the information you may find in this reading.

_____ an aptitude test  _____ career choices

_____ movie listings  _____ a personal information record

**B.** Read the following selection from the reading and the questions below. Circle the letter of the correct answer for each question.

*Los estudiantes que vienen al centro, pueden...*
* *investigar diferentes carreras*
* *buscar información sobre cientos de universidades*
* *asistir a presentaciones sobre cómo financiar los estudios*

1. What can a student do at the Career Center?
   **a.** find out about careers and universities
   **b.** find out about restaurants

2. About how many universities can students find information?
   **a.** less than 100 universities
   **b.** more than 100 universities

3. What can students learn at the presentations offered by the Career Center?
   **a.** how to finance their education
   **b.** how to become involved in sports or clubs

**C.** Fill out the following **portafolio personal** by using either your own information or made-up information.

Nombre: _____

Dirección: _____

Grado: _____ Intereses extracurriculares: _____

_____

Universidades que me interesan: _____

_____

# Presentación oral (p. 475)

**Task:** Prepare a presentation to a partner about a job you might expect to have in the future. Explain why you would choose that job.

**A.** Charts can help you organize information for a presentation. Think about classes you like and, in the first column, fill in the two subjects you prefer. In the second column, list two activities that you enjoy doing. The first line is done for you as an example.

| Cursos favoritos | Diversiones |
|---|---|
| la literatura | leer libros |
|  |  |
|  |  |

**B.** Use your answers from **part A** and the list of professions below, or choose another profession you have learned about in this chapter to complete the sentences.

| | | | |
|---|---|---|---|
| contador, -a | veterinario, -a | abogado, -a | gerente |
| arquitecto, -a | ingeniero, -a | profesor, -a | pintor, -a |

Mis clases favoritas son _____ y _____.

Las actividades que más me gustan son _____ y _____.

Estudiaré para ser _____ porque me gusta _____.

**C.** Read your statements from **part B** to practice for the oral presentation. Practice your presentation several times. Try to:

- provide as much information as you can
- speak clearly

**D.** Tell your partner about your interests and what you plan to do in the future.

Write the Spanish vocabulary word below each picture. Be sure to include the article for each noun.

**Capítulo 9B**

Fecha _____  **Vocabulary Flash Cards, Sheet 2**

Write the Spanish vocabulary word below each picture. If there is a word or phrase, copy it in the space provided. Be sure to include the article for each noun.

_____

_____

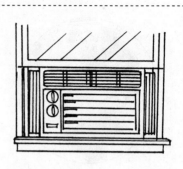

_____

_____

_____

_____

**la calefacción**

_____

**económico, económica**

_____,

_____

**eficiente**

_____

**Capítulo 9B**

Copy the word or phrase in the space provided. Be sure to include the article for each noun.

| | | |
|---|---|---|
| **la electricidad**<br><br>_____<br>_____ | **la energía**<br><br>_____<br>_____ | **conservar**<br><br><br>_____ |
| **contra**<br><br><br>_____ | **la destrucción**<br><br>_____<br>_____ | **ecológico, ecológica**<br><br>_____ ,<br>_____ |
| **eliminar**<br><br><br>_____ | **en peligro de extinción**<br><br>_____ _____<br>_____ | **la fuente**<br><br>_____<br>_____ |

Copy the word or phrase in the space provided. Be sure to include the article for each noun.

| | | |
|---|---|---|
| **funcionar** | **grave** | **juntarse** |
| _____ | _____ | _____ |
| **luchar** | **la manera** | **el medio ambiente** |
| _____ | _____ | _____ _____ |
| **mejorar** | **proteger** | **puro, pura** |
| | | _____ , |
| _____ | _____ | _____ |

Copy the word or phrase in the space provided. Be sure to include the article for each noun.

| reducir | resolver | además (de) |
|---|---|---|
| _____ | _____ | _____ |
| dudar | es cierto | haya |
| _____ | ___ ___ | _____ |
| ahorrar | la naturaleza | contaminado, contaminada |
| _____ | _____ | _____, _____ |

**Capítulo 9B**

These blank cards can be used to write and practice other Spanish vocabulary for the chapter.

|  |  |  |
| --- | --- | --- |
| _____ | _____ | _____ |
| _____ | _____ | _____ |
| _____ | _____ | _____ |

Tear out this page. Write the English words on the lines. Fold the paper along the dotted line to see the correct answers so you can check your work.

la naturaleza _____

el bosque _____

el desierto _____

la selva tropical _____

el aire
acondicionado _____

la calefacción _____

la electricidad _____

la energía _____

conservar _____

la contaminación _____

contaminado,
contaminada _____

la destrucción _____

ecológico, ecológica _____

el medio ambiente _____

Fold In

Tear out this page. Write the Spanish words on the lines. Fold the paper along the dotted line to see the correct answers so you can check your work.

nature _____

forest _____

desert _____

rain forest _____

air conditioning _____

heat _____

electricity _____

energy _____

to conserve _____

pollution _____

polluted _____

destruction _____

ecological _____

environment _____

Fold In ←

**Capítulo 9B**

Tear out this page. Write the English words on the lines. Fold the paper along the dotted line to see the correct answers so you can check your work.

el espacio                          _____

la Luna                             _____

la Tierra                           _____

económico,                          _____
económica

eficiente                           _____

contra                              _____

en peligro                          _____
de extinción

funcionar                           _____

luchar                              _____

mejorar                             _____

reducir                             _____

además (de)                         _____

dudar                               _____

proteger                            _____

Fold In

Tear out this page. Write the Spanish words on the lines. Fold the paper along the dotted line to see the correct answers so you can check your work.

(outer) space _____

the moon _____

Earth _____

economical _____

efficient _____

against _____

endangered, in danger of extinction _____

to function, to work _____

to fight _____

to improve _____

to reduce _____

in addition (to), besides _____

to doubt _____

to protect _____

Fold In

**Capítulo 9B**   Fecha _____

# The future tense: other irregular verbs (p. 490)

- Other verbs that have irregular stems in the future tense are:

  decir → dir-           querer → querr-        salir → saldr-
  poner → pondr-                                venir → vendr-

- Here is the future tense of the verb **querer**:

| QUERER | | | |
|---|---|---|---|
| yo | **querré** | nosotros/nosotras | **querremos** |
| tú | **querrás** | vosotros/vosotras | **querréis** |
| usted/él/ella | **querrá** | ustedes/ellos/ellas | **querrán** |

**A.** Look at each sentence and write the infinitive form of the underlined verb.

**Modelo**   Ellos <u>dirán</u> que nuestro valle es bonito. *Infinitive:* ___*decir*___

1. Nosotros <u>pondremos</u> plantas en las salas de clases. *Infinitive:* _____

2. Yo <u>querré</u> conservar la naturaleza. *Infinitive:* _____

3. Los turistas no <u>vendrán</u> a nuestro pueblo. *Infinitive:* _____

4. Tú <u>saldrás</u> a luchar contra la contaminación. *Infinitive:* _____

5. Ustedes <u>dirán</u> que el agua está contaminada. *Infinitive:* _____

**B.** Complete the following exchanges by writing the correct future form of the verb in parentheses. Follow the model.

**Modelo**   PEDRO: ¿Qué ___*dirán*___ ustedes del medio ambiente? (**decir**)

ILIANA: Nosotros ___*diremos*___ que está muy contaminado. (**decir**)

1. PEDRO: ¿Cuándo _____ ustedes al bosque? (**salir**)

   ILIANA: Nosotros _____ por la mañana. (**salir**)

2. PEDRO: ¿Qué _____ hacer tú para proteger el medio ambiente? (**querer**)

   ILIANA: Yo _____ usar la energía solar. (**querer**)

3. PEDRO: ¿Tu hermana _____ más plantas en la casa? (**poner**)

   ILIANA: Sí, y ella también _____ flores. (**poner**)

4. PEDRO: ¿Ella _____ con nosotros a proteger la selva tropical? (**venir**)

   ILIANA: Sí, ella y mis hermanos _____. (**venir**)

Nombre _____     Hora _____

**Capítulo 9B**

Fecha _____

**Guided Practice Activities 9B-2**

# The future tense: other irregular verbs (*continued*)

**C.** Look at the pictures and read the sentences. Then, look at the verb choices in parentheses and complete each sentence with the appropriate future form of the verb you choose. Follow the model.

**Modelo**  Tú ____*querrás*____ reducir la contaminación.  ( **querer / salir** )

**1.** Ellos no _____ destruir el bosque.  ( **querer / venir** )

**2.** Nosotros _____ que debemos conservar energía en nuestra casa.  ( **querer / decir** )

**3.** Todos los estudiantes _____ en bicicleta para reducir la contaminación del aire.  ( **venir / poner** )

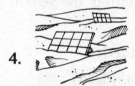

**4.** Nosotros _____ energía solar en nuestras casas.  ( **salir / poner** )

**5.** Si hay demasiada contaminación en la Tierra, Federico _____ al espacio.  ( **salir / venir** )

# The present subjunctive with expressions of doubt (p. 493)

- In the same way that the subjunctive is used with impersonal expressions and to communicate a desire to influence someone else's actions, it is also used after verbs and expressions of doubt or uncertainty. Some expressions of doubt or uncertainty are:

| | |
|---|---|
| **dudar que** | *to doubt that* |
| **no es cierto que** | *it is not certain that* |
| **no creer que** | *to not believe that* |
| **no estar seguro, -a de que** | *to be unsure that* |
| **es imposible que** | *it is impossible that* |
| **es posible que** | *it is possible that* |

> **No es cierto que puedan proteger el medio ambiente.**
> *It is not certain that they can protect the environment.*

**A.** In the sentences below, underline the expressions that indicate uncertainty or doubt. Then, circle the verbs in the subjunctive form. The first one is done for you.

1. <u>Es imposible que</u> nosotros no (cuidemos) la Tierra.

2. Dudo que nosotros no luchemos contra la contaminación.

3. Es posible que muchos animales estén en peligro de extinción.

4. No es cierto que en nuestra casa usemos mucha energía.

5. Nosotros no creemos que ellos no cuiden la colina.

6. No estoy seguro de que los bosques se conserven bien.

7. Es imposible que nosotros no protejamos la naturaleza.

# The present subjunctive with expressions of doubt (*continued*)

- While the subjunctive is used to show uncertainty, the indicative is used to show certainty. Compare these sentences:

  **No es cierto que ellas ahorren energía.** *It is not certain that they will save energy.*
  **Es cierto que ellos ahorran energía.** *It is certain that they are saving energy.*

**B.** Read the following sentences and underline the expressions of doubt or certainty. If the expression indicates certainty, write **C**. If it indicates doubt or uncertainty, write **D**. Follow the models.

**Modelo 1**  <u>Es verdad que</u> tenemos que reducir la contaminación. *C*

**Modelo 2**  <u>No es verdad que</u> tengamos que reciclar. *D*

1. No creemos que el aire esté contaminado. _____

2. Estamos seguros de que muchos animales están en peligro de extinción. _____

3. Creo que la energía solar es muy eficiente. _____

4. No estoy seguro de que sea económico usar la calefacción. _____

5. Es cierto que los problemas ecológicos se resuelven. _____

6. Creo que debemos conservar energía. _____

**C.** Circle the correct form of the verbs in parentheses to complete each sentence. Use the expression of doubt or certainty in each sentence to choose whether you circle the present subjunctive or the present indicative.

1. Yo estoy seguro de que nosotros ( **podamos** / **podemos** ) cuidar la Tierra.

2. Mis profesores creen que los niños de hoy ( **trabajan** / **trabajen** ) mucho para conservar energía.

3. Es imposible que los Estados Unidos ( **usa** / **use** ) menos energía que otros países.

4. Dudamos que tú ( **estés** / **estás** ) preocupado por la conservación de los bosques.

5. Es cierto que Uds. ( **quieren** / **quieran** ) resolver los problemas ecológicos.

6. No es cierto que los norteamericanos ( **destruyan** / **destruyen** ) los bosques.

# The present subjunctive with expressions of doubt (*continued*)

- The subjunctive form of **hay** is **haya,** from the verb **haber:**

  **Es posible que haya suficiente electricidad.**
  *It is possible that **there is** enough electricity.*

**D.** Complete the sentences by writing either the indicative form **hay** or the subjunctive form **haya.** Follow the model.

**Modelo**   ¿No crees que ___*haya*___ un problema grave?

1. Dudamos que _____ una fuente de energía nueva.

2. Es cierto que _____ mucha destrucción en las selvas tropicales.

3. Él está seguro de que _____ una manera de reducir la contaminación.

4. Es imposible que _____ vida en el espacio.

5. Es posible que _____ desiertos en la Luna.

**E.** Complete the following advertisement with the subjunctive or the indicative form of the verbs given. The first one is done for you.

¿Dudas que tu ayuda _____*sea*_____ (**ser**) importante para la Tierra? ¿No estás

seguro de que los humanos _____ (**poder**) hacer cambios importantes para

la naturaleza? Debes visitar el parque zoológico Las Palmas. Aquí sabrás que ¡es cierto

que nosotros _____ (**trabajar**) para los animales que están en peligro de

extinción! ¡Es posible que una corporación grande _____ (**conservar**) agua

y energía! ¡Es imposible que tú no _____ (**ayudar**) a la causa! En el

zoológico Las Palmas, sabemos que tú _____ (**ir**) a divertirte. Creemos que

tú y tu familia _____ (**proteger**) la naturaleza mientras observan los

animales. Juntos, es posible que nosotros _____ (**luchar**) contra la

extinción.

# Lectura: Protejamos la Antártida (pp. 498–499)

**A.** When you read an article, you should be aware that the writer may have strong opinions about the issues. Identify and circle the words below that indicate an opinion.

Dudo...               Hay...                Sabemos...

Es peligroso...       Es importante...      Se llama...

**B.** Read the following paragraph from the article in your textbook. You may not know some of the words and phrases below from the article. Try to determine the meaning of them from their context in the paragraph and from what you already know about the Antarctic.

> *¡Estamos en peligro!*
>
> *Las regiones polares son muy importantes para la supervivencia de la Tierra entera. Los casquetes de hielo en las zonas polares reflejan luz solar y así regularizan la temperatura de la Tierra. Cuando se destruyen estos casquetes, hay menos luz solar que se refleja y la Tierra se convierte en un receptor termal. Esto se llama el efecto de invernadero. Es en la Antártida que en 1985 se reportaron por primera vez los hoyos en la capa del ozono y aquí es donde hoy día se trata de encontrar una solución.*

1. casquetes de hielo      **a.** holes              **b.** ice caps

2. efecto de invernadero   **a.** greenhouse effect  **b.** point of departure

3. supervivencia           **a.** abundance          **b.** survival

4. hoyos                   **a.** holes              **b.** scientific teams

5. capa del ozono          **a.** rules              **b.** ozone layer

**C.** Determine the author's point of view in the paragraph in **part B** by circling the letter of the correct ending for each sentence.

1. Según el título, el autor cree que _____
   **a.** todo va bien.
   **b.** todo no va bien.

2. El autor cree que las regiones polares _____
   **a.** son importantes para la Tierra.
   **b.** no sirven para nada.

3. Es posible que el autor piense que _____
   **a.** es necesario resolver el problema de los hoyos en la capa del ozono.
   **b.** los hoyos en la capa del ozono son buenos para la Tierra.

# Presentación escrita (p. 501)

**Task:** Write an article for the daily paper explaining your volunteer project to improve your community.

**A.** Choose a volunteer project from the box or write one that you would like to do in your community.

> • recoger basura en un parque
>
> • comenzar un programa para reciclar periódicos viejos
>
> • ahorrar dinero para proteger a los animales en peligro de extinción
>
> • _____

**B.** Based on the project you chose in **part A**, complete the following sentences by circling one of the options listed.

1. Para este proyecto trabajaré

   **a.** todos los días.          **b.** los fines de semana.

2. Pueden participar

   **a.** personas mayores.          **b.** todas las personas.

3. Es importante porque

   **a.** protegemos el medio ambiente.          **b.** ayudamos a las personas.

**C.** Use your answers from **part B** to answer the following questions about your volunteer project. You may use the model to help you.

| Modelo | |
|---|---|
| ¿Qué ...? | *Me gustaría recoger basura en un parque.* |
| ¿Quién(es)...? | *Mis amigos y yo vamos a trabajar juntos.* |
| ¿Por qué...? | *Queremos tener un medio ambiente limpio y sano.* |
| ¿Dónde...? | *Vamos a trabajar en el parque del centro de la ciudad.* |
| ¿Cuándo...? | *Trabajaremos todos los fines de semana durante el verano.* |

1. ¿Qué...? _____

2. ¿Quién(es)...? _____

3. ¿Por qué...? _____

4. ¿Dónde...? _____

5. ¿Cuándo...? _____

**D.** Use your answers in **part C** to write your article. Check for correct spelling, verb forms, and vocabulary, and rewrite your article if necessary.

# Notes

344

**Vocabulary Flash Cards**

*Guided Practice Activities* ━ *Vocabulary Flash Cards*

*Guided Practice Activities* ━ *Vocabulary Flash Cards*

Nombre

Hora

Fecha

**Vocabulary Flash Cards**

*Guided Practice Activities* — *Vocabulary Flash Cards*

Nombre _____

Hora _____

Fecha _____

**Vocabulary Flash Cards**

**Vocabulary Flash Cards**